THE NEW Soul Food COOKBOOK

for People with Diabetes

by
FABIOLA DEMPS GAINES
and
RONIECE WEAVER

American Diabetes Association

Book Acquisitions	Robert J. Anthony
Editor	Laurie Guffey
Production Director	Carolyn R. Segree
Production Coordinator	Peggy M. Rote
Composition	Harlowe Typography, Inc.
Text and Cover Design	Wickham & Associates, Inc.
Nutrient Analysis	Nutritional Computing Concepts, Inc.

Printed in the United States of America
5 7 9 10 8 6 4 2

The suggestions and information contained in this publication are generally consistent with the *Clinical Practice Recommendations* and other policies of the American Diabetes Association, but they do not represent the policy or position of the Association or any of its boards or committees. Reasonable steps have been taken to ensure the accuracy of the information presented. However, the American Diabetes Association cannot ensure the safety or efficacy of any product or service described in this publication. Individuals are advised to consult a physician or other appropriate health care professional before undertaking any diet or exercise program or taking any medication referred to in this publication. Professionals must use and apply their own professional judgment, experience, and training and should not rely solely on the information contained in this publication before prescribing any diet, exercise, or medication. The American Diabetes Association—its officers, directors, employees, volunteers, and members—assumes no responsibility or liability for personal or other injury, loss, or damage that may result from the suggestions or information in this publication.

ADA titles may be purchased for business or promotional use or for special sales. To purchase this book in large quantities, or for custom editions of this book with your logo, contact Lee Romano Sequeira, Special Sales & Promotions, at the address below, or at LRomano@diabetes.org or 703-299-2046.

American Diabetes Association
1701 N. Beauregard St.
Alexandria, Virginia 22311

On the cover (left to right): Rogelle's Shrimp Creole (p. 80), Baked Acorn Squash (p. 91), Corn Muffins (p. 121), Soul Slaw (p. 156), Rojean's Cornish Hens (p. 63), and Sweet Potato Pie (p. 195).

Library of Congress Cataloging-in-Publication Data

Weaver, Roniece, 1960–
    The new soul food cookbook for people with diabetes / Roniece
Weaver and Fabiola Gaines.
        p.   cm.
    Includes index.
    ISBN 1-58040-008-6 (pbk.)
      1. Diabetes—Diet therapy—Recipes.   2. Afro-American cookery.
I. Gaines, Fabiola, 1952–   .   II. Title.
RC662.W346   1999
616.4'620654–dc21
                                              99-12172
                                                CIP

To my parents, Bernetha Sirmans Demps and John L. Demps, Sr. Your spirits will be forever with me.

—FDG

To Dad and Mom. Daddy, I know you're not here to see my joy, but your spirit is alive and well in me. Thank you for your inspirational thoughts and words of encouragement. Mom, you are truly the best. Thank you for listening to me and being a stabilizing force. God has blessed me, in that I have come into this world through the both of you.

—RW

ontents

Preface

IT'S HARD FOR US TO THINK OF ANYONE WE KNOW who hasn't been touched by diabetes in some way, either personally or through a family member. Diabetes represents one of the great health problems of our community. We have spent years learning how to help people with diabetes develop healthier ways of eating, but before that, we were children in homes where diabetes was an unwelcome presence. We have lived much of what you may be living now, and we know it's not easy to make some of the changes you want to make.

Roniece remembers when her dad suddenly began to eat more sweets and complain of tiredness and blurry vision. Everyone tried to ignore these signs, until the day her dad didn't get up to go to work. He was told to go on insulin, a special diet, and exercise. The first Sunday morning after diagnosis, as he reached for the familiar biscuits, butter, bacon, and syrup, Roniece began to cry. Her father looked at her in amazement. "I'm the one who should be crying, not you!" he said, "Everybody has taken everything I love away from me!" But he left the table without eating more.

Fabiola's father was diagnosed with diabetes after a heart attack, but he was determined to avoid insulin shots. She watched as he struggled to come to terms with the inadequate instructions he was given on diet and exercise. The rest of the family had to do without favorite sweets and desserts, until the day her mother made her special sweet potato pie and served her dad a piece. He objected, asking, "Are you trying to kill me? That pie is not on my meal plan!" After a year, her dad was controlling his diabetes through diet and exercise alone, and Fabiola was learning how far a little determination and education could help someone go.

There are millions of people in our community with undiagnosed diabetes. Worse, there are those who know they have diabetes and aren't willing or don't know how to make the small changes necessary to take care of themselves. We wrote this book to help you learn how you can eat better without giving up some of the traditional flavors you love. We want you to know you can live long, healthy lives, even with a condition like diabetes. That's within your power. You have the strength to meet this challenge. We hope you will enjoy these recipes for many, many years.

Acknowledgments

This cookbook would not have been possible without the love and support of many people. Thank you for assisting me in this endeavor. Your time, patience, and recipes have been invaluable. I thank my soul mate, Charlie A. Gaines, III, whom I love for many reasons. If not for your guidance, support, teaching, and reasoning I would have given up. You kept me going through those late-night sessions. Thank you for being the wonderful man you are. I want to thank my adult children (I know you wanted me to put that in), Devona and Tramaine, for the many times you just left me alone. You are wonderful children and I am so proud of both of you. My mother-in-law, Mary Alice Gaines, kept me on my toes while trying to keep her blood sugars under control. Thank you for your prayers and guidance these past years. Thanks to Audrey Allison for the long, tireless nights of typing while we worked on revisions. I thank my siblings, John L. Demps, Jr., Jeanette Demps Hudson, and Eunice Demps, for the memories of stress-free days and laughter. Thanks to Cynthia Holmes for believing in me. I appreciate the support and love of my aunts and uncles on the Demps, Holmes, and Sirmans sides of the family. Deborah Jean Mitchell, Vavescia Johnson, Felecia Williams, and Almeda Jefferson, thank you for being the best friends a girl could have. Thanks to the American Diabetes Association of Orlando for believing in us and giving us the opportunity to make a difference in our community. And thanks to the American Diabetes Association, National Center, for the freedom to create this book and for giving us the chance to get the message out.

—FDG

My heartfelt thanks to my husband, Dr. Curtis Weaver, for reading this book and lending a strong shoulder so I could finish it. Thanks also to the loves of my life, my children, Candace and Curtis (CJ), for giving me the time I needed to be alone. Thanks to my sisters, Willa Ashe, Althea Howell, and Rojean Williams, for your input and words of encouragement. You all have been an irreplaceable cheerleading section. Thanks to my loving in-laws and friends, Zelma Weaver, Isabella Christian, Michael Weaver, Julia Weaver, Everette Howell, and Daughn Cantrell, for sharing your family recipes and experiences with diabetes. (Mike and Everette: it's not the end of the world—you can meet the challenge of living with diabetes.) Glenn Barbour, thanks for the many times you inspired me to continue with this project. Your energy is contagious and it helped me through many book pages. I thank the Reverend Walter R. Prince, pastor of Mt. Pleasant Missionary Baptist Church of Orlando, Florida, for your spiritual guidance and uplifting words that inspire me to continue to grow and help me be creative. You have taught me to have faith and believe that through God, all things are possible. Thank you for the hours you gave to this book. I appreciate the support of the Mt. Pleasant Missionary Baptist Church family and the opportunity to work with the congregation, Silver Angels, and many other projects. I am proud to say that my church home is one that practices "heart healthy" deeds of service. Thanks to Deaconesses Della Fayson and Mary Key, Deacon Perry Bell, and Bishop Simon Peter Mabson, for sharing your stories with me. Sherman Sheffield made us look great in print—you're the best. Lorraine Onfroy, CDE; the American Diabetes Association in Orlando; Delia Javier; and Nancy Carlton offered their kind support from the very beginning. We continue to appreciate their input and assistance. The Orlando Regional Medical Center Diabetes Treatment Center of Orlando offered clinical opinions and thoughtful revisions. Thanks for the collaborative input. God put Parniece Spears and Edward J. Thompson in my path at a special time in my life. Thank you for your friendship. My deepest appreciation goes to my many special friends who were there for late-night talks or e-mail conversations. You are all jewels that will always shine in the window to my heart. I love you all.

—RW

A Note about Food Labels

MANY FOOD LABELS IN THE GROCERY STORE use terms that can be confusing. To help you shop and eat better, here is a list of the common terms as defined by the Food and Drug Administration.

Sugar

Sugar Free: Less than 0.5 grams of sugar per serving.

No Added Sugar, Without Added Sugar, No Sugar Added: This does not mean the same as "sugar free." A label bearing these words means that no sugars were added during processing, or that processing does not increase the sugar content above the amount the ingredients naturally contain. Consult the nutrition information panel to see the total amount of sugar in this product.

Reduced Sugar: At least 25% less sugar per serving than the regular product.

Calories

Calorie Free: Fewer than 5 calories per serving.

Low Calorie: 40 calories or less per serving. (If servings are smaller than 30 grams, or smaller than 2 tablespoons, this means 40 calories or less per 50 grams of food.)

Reduced Calorie, Fewer Calories: At least 25% fewer calories per serving than the regular product.

Fat

Fat Free, Nonfat: Less than 0.5 grams of fat per serving.

Low Fat: 3 grams or less of fat per serving. (If servings are smaller than 30 grams, or smaller than 2 tablespoons, this means 3 grams or less of fat per 50 grams of food.)

Reduced Fat, Less Fat: At least 25% less fat per serving than the regular product.

Cholesterol

Cholesterol Free: Less than 2 milligrams of cholesterol, and 2 grams or less of saturated fat per serving.

Low Cholesterol: 20 milligrams or less of cholesterol, and 2 grams or less of saturated fat per serving.

Reduced Cholesterol, Less Cholesterol: At least 25% less cholesterol, and 2 grams or less of saturated fat per serving than the regular product.

Sodium

Sodium Free: Less than 5 milligrams of sodium per serving.

Low Sodium: 140 milligrams or less of sodium per serving.

Very Low Sodium: 35 milligrams or less of sodium per serving.

Reduced Sodium, Less Sodium: At least 25% less sodium per serving than the regular product.

Light or Lite Foods

Foods that are labeled "Light" or "Lite" are usually either lower in fat or lower in calories than the regular product. Some products may also be lower in sodium. Check the nutrition information label on the back of the product to make sure.

Meat and Poultry

Lean: Less than 10 grams of fat, 4.5 grams or less of saturated fat, and less than 95 milligrams of cholesterol per serving and per 100 grams.

Extra Lean: Less than 5 grams of fat, less than 2 grams of saturated fat, and less than 95 milligrams of cholesterol per serving and per 100 grams.

The New Soul Food Cookbook

*I*ntroduction

THE TRADITION OF AFRICAN AMERICAN COOKERY is a long one, steeped in ancient history, recent tribulation, and abiding faith. From its roots in grain-producing civilizations in Egypt, through its transformation by contact with European cultures, and during its wrenching evolution caused by the largest forced uprooting of a group of people that has ever occurred in history, African American culture has survived, nowhere more obviously than in its cuisine.

African slaves became the gardeners and cooks of the southern plantations, and once freed, migrated north and west to work as chuck wagon cooks, railroad chefs, nightclub hosts, and restaurant owners. New geographical influences were integrated into old traditions, methods, and techniques to create constantly evolving flavor combinations. Other recipes were passed on from generation to generation, and remained virtually unchanged for hundreds of years. Modern soul food cooking represents the best of the melding of old and new, of past and present food practices.

When the first slaves arrived in Virginia in 1619, it was a matter of survival to take whatever scraps were available and make them palatable. Common foods included rice, beans, cornmeal, black-eyed peas, sweet potatoes (which replaced the African yam), greens and onions grown in backyard gardens, okra, chiles from the Caribbean (a cheap way to add flavor to food), meat scraps (usually "fatback" from hogs), and molasses.

Diets were predominantly vegetarian, with some fish, possum, or squirrel for flavor. Foods were boiled, fried, roasted, or baked. Stews and thick gumbos, the liberal use of molasses, and fat-laden gravies provided calories. African Americans used salt

1

and sweeteners in abundance, suffering no ill effects from this excess due to the countless hours spent in hard manual labor.

The strong tradition of the family established in Africa abides today in shared meals at home, church, and restaurants, where the cooking is often collective and the food sustains the spirit as well as the body. But modern African Americans have new health concerns not shared by their ancestors. The liberal use of salt and sweeteners in foods prepared traditionally is killing us. We can avoid much of the hypertension, heart disease, and diabetes plaguing us through simple modifications to our meal plans and cooking styles. If you've been diagnosed with diabetes, we'll show you how to make easy changes to your soul food with losing too much of the flavor and tradition you love.

Accepting the Truth

The first thing you need to do is accept the fact that you have diabetes. A diagnosis of diabetes does not mean the end of life as you know it—only that, with some lifestyle changes, you can prevent some of the scary complications that may have afflicted some of your loved ones. It's common to feel angry, depressed, or disbelieving when you first learn you have diabetes. Accepting the truth means working through these feelings in order to take care of yourself and live a full life.

If you find yourself saying "one bite won't hurt," "this sore will heal by itself," "I'll go to the doctor later," "my diabetes isn't serious," or "I only take pills, not insulin," you could be in denial about diabetes. Try talking to other people about how they cope with their diabetes. Tell your friends and family what you need to do to take care of yourself. Accept that it may take some time to adapt to this news.

If you're angry or depressed, try some ways to defuse your feelings. Move around, breathe deeply, go see a movie, go for a walk with a loved one. Talk about it with someone, or try to see the larger picture. Let your depression fade, and your anger make you stronger, more determined to become healthier.

What Is Diabetes?

Diabetes is a disorder caused by lack of a hormone called insulin, which is made in the pancreas. This can happen when the pancreas is not making enough insulin, or when the cells of the body are not able to use it. Insulin is used to capture the glucose (sugar) circulating in your bloodstream and bring it into your cells. Glucose is broken down from the food you eat and used for energy. If there is not enough insulin, too much glucose stays in your blood. You will feel tired, your body may begin to get damaged from the high levels of glucose in your blood, and you will feel thirsty and need to urinate more often, which is your body's attempt to reduce the levels of glucose in your bloodstream.

There are two main types of diabetes, type 1 and type 2. In type 1 diabetes, which is sometimes called juvenile-onset diabetes or insulin-dependent diabetes, your body makes little or no insulin. This type usually occurs early in life and is seen more often in children and young adults. People with type 1 diabetes must take regular injections of insulin to stay healthy.

Type 2 diabetes is sometimes known as non-insulin-dependent or adult-onset diabetes. Type 2 diabetes is the most common type of diabetes and is very common among African Americans. Most people with type 2 diabetes make some insulin; however, the amount of insulin is not sufficient or the body cannot use what it does make. Luckily, many people who have type 2 diabetes can control it with a healthy diet and exercise. Some people may need pills and/or insulin injections to help control their diabetes.

Complications of Diabetes

Type 1 and type 2 diabetes can cause many long-term problems. These problems are created by elevated blood glucose over a long period of time, and may include blindness; kidney disease; nerve impairment; heart disease; stroke; amputations; and other problems with the skin, feet, gums, and sexual function.

In most cases, with careful meal planning, exercise, and medication; regular visits to your doctor; and working with your health care team to adjust your self-care plan, you can avoid the worst of these complications and live a long and healthy life.

Hypoglycemia

If you have diabetes you may experience hypoglycemia. This condition occurs when your blood glucose level falls too low, usually because of too much insulin or exercise or not enough food. Some medications you might take for other conditions can cause blood glucose to drop, as can alcohol.

This condition can sneak up on you quickly. It is important to treat hypoglycemia as soon as possible, because it can cause illness in a short period of time that can result in unconsciousness or a seizure. The symptoms of hypoglycemia include:

- Shakiness
- Dizziness
- Sweating
- Hunger
- Headache
- Pale skin color
- Sudden moodiness
- Clumsy or jerking movements
- Confusion or trouble paying attention
- Tingling sensation around the mouth
- Loss of consciousness
- Seizures

A quick way to treat low blood glucose is by drinking something with sugar in it, such as juice or non-diet soda, eating some glucose tablets or candy, or drinking a glass of milk. Consult your doctor to find out the best way for you to treat a hypoglycemic reaction. If you are taking insulin, make sure you always have something with you to treat hypoglycemia.

It would be wise to tell family members, coworkers, and friends that you have diabetes. It's important for them to understand how to react to situations when you are not feeling well. One of them may save your life when you are in a crisis. You may want to buy an ID bracelet advising strangers about your diabetes.

If someone loses consciousness or experience seizures, be sure someone knows to call Emergency Services (911). A person who faints from hypoglycemia needs immediate treatment, such as an injection of glucagon or emergency treatment in a hospital. You should be taken to the hospital if you do not respond to your first series of treatment efforts (drinking juice or soda) or if you are suffering a seizure.

Hyperglycemia

People with diabetes can also develop a condition known as hyperglycemia. This is when the body has too much glucose in the blood. Hyperglycemia can be caused by not taking enough medication, stopping regular exercise abruptly, overeating, stress or illness, or a combination of these factors.

Hyperglycemia (high blood glucose) is the opposite of hypoglycemia (low blood glucose). Hyperglycemia develops at a slower pace. It generally develops in several hours or even days. High blood glucose produces ketones (byproducts of your body's effort to burn fat instead of glucose for fuel). You can measure the ketone level of your blood to see if you have hyperglycemia. A very serious form of hyperglycemia leads to a condition called DKA, diabetic ketoacidosis, which can cause a coma. The symptoms of hyperglycemia include:

- Extreme thirst
- Frequent urination
- Tiredness
- Difficulty breathing
- Blurred vision
- Vomiting or upset stomach
- Headache
- Dry, itchy skin
- Weight loss
- Fruity smell on breath (from the ketones)

Mild hyperglycemia is treated with extra insulin, additional exercise, or less food at the next meal or snack. More serious hyperglycemia requires a doctor's care.

Now What?

You meet with your doctor to learn all you can about your individual condition. Your doctor will refer you to a dietitian, who will help you plan meals and snacks to optimize your health. You'll learn how to measure your own blood glucose level so you can identify hypoglycemia and hyperglycemia. You'll want to begin an easy exercise program and stop smoking. Your goals may include:

- Learning all you can about your diabetes from many sources, including a certified diabetes educator (CDE)

- Getting a tasty meal plan from a registered dietitian (many of whom are also CDEs)

- Maintaining a healthy weight by eating a variety of small, frequent meals

- Starting a healthy exercise routine

- Stopping unhealthy habits like smoking

- Monitoring and recording your blood glucose levels, and testing for urine ketones, if necessary

- Taking the proper medications, including insulin, if needed

- Getting annual dilated eye examinations by an ophthalmologist

- Establishing long- and short-term goals for your diabetes

Sometimes the hardest goal of all can be changing how you eat. You may believe you need to eliminate every food you love to be successful at managing your diabetes. That's just not true. You can learn to integrate many of your old favorites into your meal plan, and add new versions of foods that taste just as good as they used to.

What Can I Eat?

You can eat many of your old favorites, with just a few simple ingredient substitutions that won't change their flavor as much as you might think. For example, use smoked turkey instead of bacon with vegetables, canola oil instead of lard for fritters, and fruit spreads instead of syrup on biscuits.

You and your dietitian will come up with a meal plan that suits you, based on what you like to eat and drink, when you need to eat or take medications, how much you exercise, and your target weight. You'll learn how to reduce swings in blood glucose by eating the same amounts of foods at the same times each day. You'll feel better, look better, and have more energy following a healthy meal plan.

Help with Meal Planning

There are several tools to help you follow a successful meal plan. Three of them are the Exchange Lists, carbohydrate counting, and the Soul Food Pyramid.

Exchange Lists

These are lists of foods that have been sorted by type and amount. The American Diabetes Association and The American Dietetic Association have agreed on the recommended quantities of these foods for people on meal plans. One serving of a food on a list has about the same amount of calories, protein, fat, and carbohydrate as the other foods on the list, and can be "exchanged" or traded based on what you feel like eating.

For example, whole-wheat bread, waffles, sugar-frosted cereal, baked potatoes, and corn are all on the starch list. Your meal plan calls for a piece of toast, but you feel like eating a waffle. You can trade one for the other, as long as you pay attention to the serving size (one piece of whole-wheat toast can be traded for one reduced-fat, 4 1/2-inch-square waffle). Your dietitian can help you figure out what your total number of exchanges from all the groups should be for each day.

Carbohydrate Counting

Carbohydrates affect your blood glucose level faster than proteins or fats do. In this meal-planning tool, you count the grams of carbohydrate in the foods you eat. You don't count vegetables, meats, or fats. You can find out how much carbohydrate a food has by looking at food labels, the Exchange Lists, or books on carbohydrate counting. As with all meal-planning methods, you still need to pay attention to the total number of calories you eat.

Soul Food Pyramid

For years, the guide to healthy eating was the Basic Four Food Groups. But in 1992, the USDA changed the four groups to six, and put them into the sections of a pyramid. In 1995, the American Diabetes Association and The American Dietetic Association adapted the pyramid for people with diabetes. It's called the Diabetes Food Pyramid, and in this book it's called the Soul Food Pyramid.

Look at the pyramid on the next page. You'll see the daily number of servings to eat from five of the groups. The group with the largest number of servings is on the bottom. As you go up the pyramid, you eat more sparingly from the groups. The Soul Food Pyramid gives you a way to visualize the different types of foods in your meal plan and how much of each you should eat.

There Has To Be a Catch

There is. It's in the portion sizes. You may need to learn to serve yourself smaller amounts of the foods you like. To feel full on less, you can try drinking water with your meal, eating more fiber-rich foods like salads and whole grains, and exercising.

If you're having trouble losing weight, you may not realize how much you're eating. You might even be shocked to find out! Your dietitian will help you decide how much you should be eating each day. The following guidelines should give you a better idea of appropriate portion sizes.

Food Item	Approximate Measure
3 ounces of meat, poultry, or fish	The palm of your hand, a deck of cards, or a cassette tape
1 cup of potato, pasta, or rice	Your fist or a tennis ball
1 ounce of cheese	A pair of dice or the length of your thumb
1 medium fruit	Your fist

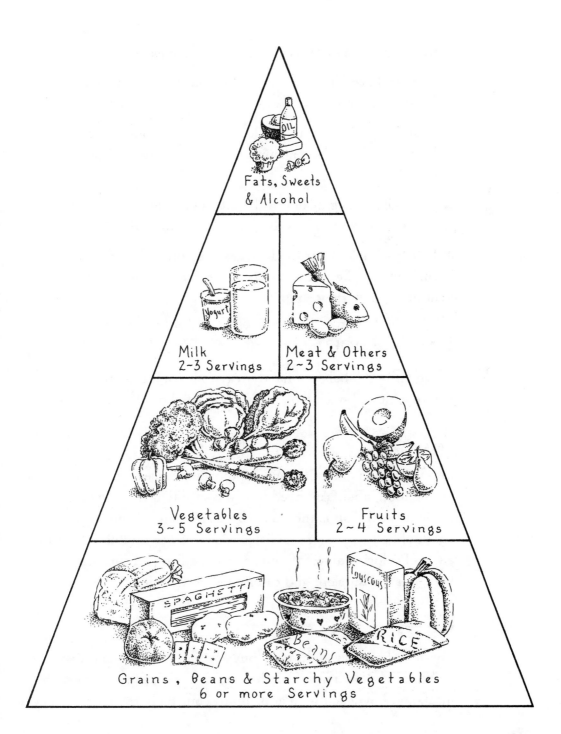

Fats, Sweets
& Alcohol

Milk
2-3 Servings

Meat & Others
2~3 Servings

Vegetables
3~5 Servings

Fruits
2~4 Servings

Grains, Beans & Starchy Vegetables
6 or more Servings

Here are some more tips to control portion size:

- Use smaller plates and dishes, so your portions won't look lost.

- Restrict your meals to one location in the house. Eating in front of the TV can encourage you to eat more without realizing it.

- Keep all serving dishes in the kitchen, instead of on the table, so you have to think before going back for more.

- Don't measure your food every time you eat. Instead, measure your dishes, bowls, and glasses once to get a general idea of how much they contain.

What Else Will Help?

Reading food labels is a handy way to learn more about what you're eating. Take a look at the food label on the next page.

Serving Size

Serving size is one of the most important pieces of information on the food label. You need to make sure that the serving size on your meal plan is the same size as the one on the label. If you eat double the serving size listed, you need to double the nutrient and calorie values. If you eat one half the serving size shown here, cut the nutrient and calorie values in half.

Calories

You may be overweight now, but you can shed the extra weight if you know how many calories you're supposed to eat at each meal, and how each food adds up to your daily total.

Total Carbohydrate

About 40–50% of your total daily calories should come from carbohydrate. Carbohydrate-rich foods are breads, potatoes, fruits, and vegetables. Choose these often! They give you nutrients and energy.

Dietary Fiber

Mama always said this would keep you "regular." Fiber is important to your diet. Fruits, vegetables, whole-grain foods, beans, and peas are all good sources of fiber and can help reduce the risk of heart disease and cancer.

Protein

Most African Americans get more protein than they need. Only about 10–20% of your

Nutrition Facts		
Serving Size 1 cup (228g)		
Servings Per Container 2		
Amount Per Serving		
Calories 260 Calories from Fat 120		
		% Daily Value*
Total Fat 13g		**20%**
Saturated Fat 5g		**25%**
Cholesterol 30mg		**10%**
Sodium 660mg		**28%**
Total Carbohydrate 31g		**10%**
Dietary Fiber 0g		**0%**
Sugars 5g		
Protein 5g		
Vitamin A 4%	•	Vitamin C 2%
Calcium 15%	•	Iron 4%

* Percent Daily Values are based on a 2,000 calorie diet. Your daily values may be higher or lower depending on your calorie needs:

	Calories:	2,000	2,500
Total Fat	Less than	65g	80g
Sat Fat	Less than	20g	25g
Cholesterol	Less than	300mg	300mg
Sodium	Less than	2,400mg	2,400mg
Total Carbohydrate		300g	375g
Dietary Fiber		25g	30g

Calories per gram:
Fat 9 • Carbohydrate 4 • Protein 4

total daily calories should come from protein. Eating red meat also means a higher intake of saturated fat and cholesterol. Eat small servings of lean meat, fish, and poultry. Try thinking of meat as a condiment to your vegetables. Use vegetable protein combinations like rice and beans instead of fatty roasts or fried foods.

Vitamins and Minerals

Don't count on one food to provide 100% of a nutrient for the day. Instead, let a combination of foods add up to a healthy daily average.

Total Fat

This is the category that gets most of us in trouble. We all need to cut back on fat! Too much fat may contribute to heart disease and cancer. Try to limit your calories from fat by using skim or low-fat milk, yogurt, and cheese. For a healthy heart, choose foods with a big difference between the total number of calories and the number of calories from fat.

Saturated Fat

This is not a new kind of fat. We know it as that fat that is visible on the different types of meat we eat. This is listed separately because it's the key player in raising blood cholesterol and increasing your risk of heart disease. Use unsaturated fats such as canola oil and olive oil instead of lard, and trim your meat carefully before cooking it.

Cholesterol

Too much dietary cholesterol may contribute to high blood cholesterol levels, implicated in heart attacks, stroke, and high blood pressure. Cut back by using egg substitutes and eating smaller servings of meat, fish, and poultry.

Sodium

We call it "salt," food labels call it "sodium." Either way, it may add up to high blood pressure in some people. Try using red pepper, herbs, and spices instead of salt to season soul food.

% Daily Value

Daily values are listed for people who eat 2,000 or 2,500 calories each day. If you eat more, your personal daily value may be higher than what's listed on the label. If you eat less, your personal daily value may be lower. For fat, saturated fat, cholesterol, and sodium, choose foods with a low % Daily Value. For dietary fiber, vitamins, and minerals, your Daily Value goal is to reach 100% of each.

What Is Your Eating Style?

How many times have you skipped breakfast because you think it's a good way to save a few calories? How many times have you skipped a meal because you were not hungry and put off eating until later in the day, when you were so hungry you overate? How many times have you found yourself following some fad diet that didn't work? Do you eat when you're lonely, angry, or depressed? Do you have difficulty resisting high-fat, high-sugar foods at family gatherings or church socials?

If so, take a careful look at your personal eating style. If you don't take a good, honest look at yourself, you will find it harder to practice healthy habits. New habits should be easy to incorporate, as long as you make specific goals and introduce small changes one at a time. Don't try to change everything all at once. Also, find what works for you. We're all different, and what worked for your neighbor, friend, or relative may not suit you.

The Food Diary

One way to examine your personal eating style is to keep a Food Diary. For one week, write down everything you eat, what time you eat, how you feel before or after eating, and how hungry you were on a scale of 1 to 10.

If you are already recording your blood glucose levels, write down your fasting values and those 2 hours after you ate. If you skip a meal or snack, write down why ("late for work," or "not hungry," for example).

After one week, meet with your dietitian or health care team and see what you can learn from the Food Diary. You may find you skip breakfast on workdays, and you're starving by 11:00 a.m. You may notice you eat more than you thought late at night in front of the TV. You may see that you're so hungry by dinnertime you stop at a fast-food restaurant because it would take too long to cook dinner.

Using this information, decide on one or two changes you want to make to improve your eating habits. You could decide to wake up 15 minutes earlier and eat some cereal in the morning, or take a leisurely walk after dinner instead of eating dessert. Continue keeping your Food Diary to document how well you're making these changes. Be patient with yourself, and you'll see your progress over time. Once these changes become a habit (usually after 6 weeks or so), begin the process again to work on other goals.

Here are some suggestions for simple changes you can make in your eating habits that will help you feel better.

- Eat breakfast! When people eat an adequate number of calories earlier in the day, they are less likely to overeat at night. Eating most of your food at night is a habit that can add extra calories and eventually increase your weight. And remember, breakfast doesn't have to consist of eggs, grits, sausage, and ham. It could be a turkey sandwich and a glass of juice.

■ You may want to plan a snack, such as a piece of fruit or glass of fat-free milk, for the late afternoon. This will slow down your urge to eat while you're making dinner. You will find that you are eating less each day if you spread out your meals and snacks throughout the day. Besides, big meals cause greater swings in blood glucose.

■ Eat about the same amount and type of food at about the same time each day, depending on your individual meal plan. This makes it easier for your body to regulate its blood glucose levels.

■ Eat slowly, appreciate each bite, and remember that your next meal or snack is only a few hours away!

Eating out

It can be hard to resist your favorite holiday, family, or restaurant foods, especially if you are already feeling deprived or upset about having diabetes. The key here is to realize you can still have almost all of your old favorites—you just need to have less of them, and enjoy them a little less often.

You can help yourself not become overwhelmed by food cravings. First, remember that your goal is to stay healthy and well. Eating a particular food is not more important than your overall health.

Second, know that you can have a little of these special occasion foods—you just need to account for them in your daily total of calories, exchanges, or carbohydrates. A dietitian can help you figure out how to do this in advance so you can go to the party or restaurant armed with your plan.

Finally, try to eat a small meal or snack before you go, so you don't arrive starving and abandon your plan.

When you go out to eat, try the following hints.

■ Go to restaurants that provide a variety of choices and alternatives.

■ Look for lighter fare on the menu, or choices marked as lower in fat or calories.

■ Don't be embarrassed to ask the waiter how the food is prepared or what the portion sizes are.

■ Ask for sauces to be served on the side.

■ Try eating early-bird specials or appetizers as entrees, both of which usually come in smaller portions.

■ Try to avoid feeling like "I paid for it, so I have to eat all of it." Your health is more important than anything else.

■ Plan your day carefully if you know you are going to have dinner away from home. Make sure you follow the rest of your meal plan.

■ Avoid "all-you-can-eat specials," as you usually will.

■ Look for words and phrases like baked, braised, broiled, cooked in its own juices, grilled, poached, roasted, steamed, and stir-fried. These cooking practices require less fat.

■ Avoid choices on the menu that say au gratin, batter-fried, fried, breaded, buttered, sauteed, with gravy, white sauce, deep-fried, french-fried, pastry, double crust, scalloped, with mayonnaise, hollandaise, pan-fried, rich, thick sauce, creamed, and crispy.

■ If you want to drink alcohol, figure out how to incorporate it into your meal plan.

■ Plan to have a little of your favorite dessert, and work out what adjustments you can make to the rest of your daily meal plan.

- Eat at a leisurely pace, and enjoy the special atmosphere.

- Build nice salads from the salad bar, but watch your choice of dressings and toppers, such as bacon, croutons, nuts, olives, and cheese.

- Avoid deluxe and super-size items when you go to drive-through restaurants—you'd be surprised by how often less is enough.

- Split your order with someone if there is too much food, or take it home and save it for another meal.

What about Alcohol?

Most people whose diabetes is under control can drink alcohol, if they drink in moderation. For our purposes, this means drinking no more than one alcoholic beverage (5 ounces of wine, 12 ounces of beer, or 1 1/2 ounces of distilled liquor) per day. If you like the flavor of alcohol but not the calories, try cooking with it. Add sherry to a marinade for meat or poultry, pour red cooking wine into a tomato sauce, or add orange liqueur to a fruit salad.

Alcohol has calories but few nutrients, and it can cause low blood glucose for those people taking insulin or other medications. People with diabetes should never drink on an empty stomach for this reason. Remember that the symptoms of too much alcohol and of hypoglycemia are very similar. You don't want people to confuse these two, because they might not give you the proper treatment when you need it.

What about Salt?

There's no doubt about it: soul food can be salty. It also tastes just as good without the salt, if you make a few simple substitutions. You'd be amazed what spices, peppers, and herbs can do for a soul food recipe. It isn't as hard as you think to retrain your taste buds to do without salt. And with the great plagues of hypertension and heart disease upon us, it's important that you do.

Sodium and salt are found mainly in processed and prepared foods. Think about the amount of salt in bacon, hot dogs, sausages, canned foods, frozen foods, cheese, pickles, mustard, salad dressing, and snack foods. But if you buy more fresh meats, grains, fruits, and vegetables, and prepare them with lemon juice, reduced-fat margarine, pepper, herbs and spices, and smoked seasoning, you will find you don't need nearly as much salt. The extra potassium found in fresh fruits and vegetables also helps lower your blood pressure.

Most people with high blood pressure need to eat 2,400 mg of sodium or less each day. To help you picture how much that is, 1/4 teaspoon of salt has 450 mg of sodium, 1 ounce of processed American cheese has 400 mg, and 8 ounces of milk has 120 mg. There are plenty of low-sodium varieties of food on the market today to help you eat less salt. Use garlic, onion, and celery powders in place of garlic, onion, and celery salt. And use fresh herbs, such as parsley and basil, whenever possible for the best flavor.

Can I Still Make My Favorite Recipes?

To use your favorite recipes in your new meal plan, try one or more of these simple adjustments.

Instead of	Use This
Bacon	Turkey bacon or sausage
Butter	Low- or reduced-fat margarine
Cheese	Low- or reduced-fat cheese
Corn chips	Baked tortilla chips
Cream cheese	Reduced-fat cream cheese
Cream	Evaporated skim milk
Creamy salad dressing	Olive oil and vinegar
Croissants	Bagels or pita bread
Egg yolks	Egg substitute
Fried chicken	Grilled or baked chicken
Fried fish	Baked fish
Fried foods	Baked, roasted, or grilled meats
Ground beef	Lean ground beef
Ground turkey	Ground turkey breast
Ham hocks	Smoked turkey or liquid smoke
Heavy sauces	Light broths
High-fat meats	Trimmed or lean meats
Ice cream	Sherbet or low-fat ice cream
Jelly, jam, or syrups	Fruit spreads
Mayonnaise	Low- or reduced-fat mayonnaise
Pork chops	Pork tenderloin
Potato chips	Pretzels
Salt pork	Smoked turkey
Sour cream	Plain yogurt or fat-free sour cream
Sugary cereals	Whole-grain cereals
Tuna packed in oil	Tuna packed in water
Vegetable oil, lard	Canola and olive oils or nonstick cooking spray
Whole milk	Fat-free or 1% milk

You can also use different cooking techniques to reduce the fat and calories in your food.

Remember, you will feel much better and find your diabetes much easier to control if you keep these goals in mind.

- Maintain a healthy weight
- Maintain normal ranges of blood glucose for you
- Eat smaller meals
- Eat on time
- Eat a variety of fresh foods
- Practice portion control
- Read food labels

You'll Feel Better if You . . .

There's one more thing you can do to feel great and achieve diabetes control: exercise. This doesn't mean you have to do anything drastic! The introduction of a simple walking program will do wonders for your health, energy, and state of mind.

What are the health benefits of physical activity? Research consistently shows that regular physical activity, combined with healthy eating habits, is the most efficient and reliable way to control your weight.

Regular physical activity can also help prevent several conditions, including heart disease and stroke, high blood pressure, osteoporosis, and back pain. Exercise can improve your mood and the way you feel about yourself, as well as reduce depression and anxiety and help you to better manage stress.

It doesn't matter what type of physical activity you perform—sports, planned exercise, household chores, yard work, or work-related tasks—all are beneficial. Studies show that even the most inactive people can gain significant health benefits if they accumulate thirty minutes or more of physical activity per day.

Keep these tips in mind when developing your exercise program.

- Follow a gradual approach to exercise to get the most benefits with the fewest risks. If you have not been exercising, start at a slow pace. As you become more fit, gradually increase the duration and pace of your activity.

- Choose activities that you enjoy and that fit your personality. For example, if you like team sports or group activities, choose things such as soccer or aerobics. If you prefer individual activities, choose things such as swimming or walking.

- Plan your activities for a time of day that suits your personality. If you are a morning person, exercise before you begin the rest of your day's activities. If you have more energy in the evening, plan activities that can be done at the end of the day. You will be more likely to stick to a physical activity program if it is convenient and enjoyable.

- Exercise regularly. To gain the most health benefits it is important to exercise as regularly as possible. Make sure you choose activities that will fit into your schedule.

- Exercise at a comfortable pace. For example, while jogging or walking briskly, you should still be able to have a conversation. If you do not feel normal again within 10 minutes following exercise, you are exercising too hard. Also, if you have difficulty breathing or feel faint or weak during or after exercise, you are exercising too hard.

■ Maximize your safety and comfort. Wear shoes that fit and clothes that move with you, and always exercise in a safe location. Many people walk in indoor shopping malls for exercise. Malls are climate-controlled and offer protection from bad weather.

■ Vary your activities. Choose a variety of activities so you don't get bored with any one thing.

■ Encourage your family or friends to support you and join you in your activity. If you have children, it is best to build healthy habits when they are young. When parents are active, children are more likely to be active and stay active for the rest of their lives.

■ Challenge yourself. Set short- and long-term goals. Celebrate every success, no matter how small.

What if I Just Want To Start . . . Walking?

Walking is one of the easiest ways to exercise. You can do it almost anywhere and anytime. Walking is also inexpensive—the only equipment you need is a pair of comfortable shoes. Walking will:

■ Give you more energy
■ Help you feel good
■ Help you relax
■ Reduce stress
■ Help you sleep better
■ Tone your muscles

- Help control your appetite
- Help you control your diabetes
- Increase the number of calories your body uses

Answer the following questions before you begin a walking program:

- Has your doctor ever told you that you have heart trouble?
- When you exercise, do you have pains in your chest or on your left side (neck, shoulder, or arm)?
- Do you often feel faint or have dizzy spells?
- Do you feel extremely breathless after mild activity?
- Has your doctor told you that you have high blood pressure?
- Has your doctor told you that you have bone or joint problems, such as arthritis, that could get worse if you exercise?
- Are you middle-aged and not used to a lot of exercise?
- Do you have a condition or physical reason not mentioned here that might interfere with an exercise program?

If you answered yes to any of these questions, please check with your doctor before starting a walking program or other form of exercise.

It is important to design a program that will work for you. In planning your walking program, keep the following points in mind:

- Stretch before you walk.
- Wear shoes with thick, flexible soles that will cushion your feet and absorb shock.
- Your feet and shoes should be inspected after exercising.

- Wear clothes that are right for the season. In the summer, light cotton clothes allow sweat to evaporate, which helps to keep you cool. Use layers of clothing in the winter and shed them as you warm up.

- Think of your walk in three parts. Walk slowly for 5 minutes. Increase your speed for the next 5 minutes. Finally, to cool down, walk slowly again for 5 minutes.

- Try to walk at least three times per week, and add 2 to 3 minutes per week to the fast walk portion of your program. If you walk less than three times per week, increase the fast walk more slowly.

- To avoid stiff or sore muscles or joints, start gradually. Over several weeks, begin walking faster and walking for longer periods of time.

- Consult your health care team about exercising during periods of poor glucose control.

Always keep safety in mind when you plan your route and the time of your walk.

- Walk in the daytime or at night in well-lighted areas.

- Walk with a partner or in a group.

- Avoid wearing jewelry or headphones.

- Be aware of your surroundings.

- Carry fast-acting glucose to treat low blood glucose reactions, if necessary.

Here's a sample walking program you might enjoy. Be sure to check with your physician or health care team before beginning any exercise program.

	Warm Up	Fast Walk	Cool Down	Total Time
Week 1	Walk slowly 5 min	Walk briskly 5 min	Walk slowly 5 min	15 min
Week 2	Walk slowly 5 min	Walk briskly 8 min	Walk slowly 5 min	18 min
Week 3	Walk slowly 5 min	Walk briskly 11 min	Walk slowly 5 min	21 min
Week 4	Walk slowly 5 min	Walk briskly 14 min	Walk slowly 5 min	24 min
Week 5	Walk slowly 5 min	Walk briskly 17 min	Walk slowly 5 min	27 min
Week 6	Walk slowly 5 min	Walk briskly 20 min	Walk slowly 5 min	30 min
Week 7	Walk slowly 5 min	Walk briskly 23 min	Walk slowly 5 min	33 min
Week 8	Walk slowly 5 min	Walk briskly 26 min	Walk slowly 5 min	36 min
Week 9 & beyond	Walk slowly 5 min	Walk briskly 30 min	Walk slowly 5 min	40 min

Combining healthy eating with an easy, fun exercise program will help you control your diabetes.

Mama's Favorite Beef and Pork

Althea's Beef Gumbo

Preparation time: 20 minutes
Serves 7   Serving size: 1 cup

 1 lb lean ground beef

 2 large onions, chopped

16 oz frozen white corn kernels, thawed

 1 15-oz can navy beans, rinsed and drained

 3 14 1/2-oz cans reduced-sodium stewed tomatoes, with juice

 1 10-oz pkg frozen sliced okra, thawed

 2 Tbsp chili powder

 2 1/3 cups cooked rice

1. Brown the ground beef and onion in a large soup pot or Dutch oven, stirring until the beef crumbles. Drain the beef, discarding fat.

2. Stir in the remaining ingredients except for the rice and bring the mixture to a boil over medium heat, stirring occasionally.

3. Cover and reduce the heat; simmer 20 minutes. Stir occasionally. Serve over 1/3 cup rice.

Exchanges
3 1/2 Starch
2 Lean Meat

Calories	390
Calories from Fat	92
Total Fat	10 g
Saturated Fat	3 g
Cholesterol	41 mg
Sodium	200 mg
Carbohydrate	56 g
Dietary Fiber	9 g
Sugars	11 g
Protein	22 g

Baked Pork Shoulder Hawaiian

Preparation time: 20 minutes
Serves 8   Serving size: 4 oz

2 lb lean boneless pork shoulder roast
   Salt to taste (optional)
   Pepper to taste (optional)
1/2 cup diced onion
1/4 cup diced green pepper
2 8-oz cans tomato sauce
1 Tbsp Worcestershire sauce
1/3 cup apple cider vinegar
1 8-oz can pineapple tidbits packed in their own juice
1/4 cup brown sugar
1/2 tsp dry mustard

1. Heat the oven to 350 degrees. Sprinkle the pork with salt and pepper and place in a shallow pan. Bake for 1 hour. Drain off all excess fat.

2. Meanwhile, mix the remaining ingredients together and let stand to blend flavors.

3. Pour the sauce over the pork and bake an additional 45 minutes, basting frequently.

Exchanges
1 Carbohydrate
3 Medium-Fat Meat
1/2 Fat

Calories 319
   Calories from Fat . 158
Total Fat . . . . 18 g
   Saturated Fat . . . . . . 7 g
Cholesterol . . . . 79 mg
Sodium . . . . 453 mg
Carbohydrate . . . . . . 18 g
   Dietary Fiber . . . . . . 1 g
   Sugars . . . . 15 g
Protein . . . . 22 g

Barbecue Pulled Pork

Preparation time: 10 minutes
Serves 4   Serving size: 4 oz

     1 lb boneless pork tenderloin
    1/2 tsp pepper
    1/4 tsp red pepper flakes
     1 Tbsp canola oil
     1 cup diced onion
     2 cloves garlic, minced
    1/2 cup barbecue sauce
    1/4 cup catsup
    1/4 cup water
     1 tsp vinegar

1. Heat the oven to 350 degrees. Sear the whole tenderloin on all sides in a hot, nonstick skillet. Remove from the heat and season with the pepper and red pepper flakes.

2. Cover the tenderloin with foil and bake for 25 minutes. Heat the oil in a medium saucepan and saute the onion and garlic for 5 minutes.

3. Add the barbecue sauce, catsup, water, and vinegar. Simmer for 10 minutes. Shred the pork with 2 forks. Add the pulled pork to the sauce. Serve on buns.

Exchanges
1 Carbohydrate
3 Lean Meat

Calories 230
    Calories from Fat . . 76
Total Fat . . . . 8 g
    Saturated Fat . . . . . . 0 g
Cholesterol . . . . 65 mg
Sodium . . . . 482 mg
Carbohydrate . . . . . . 13 g
    Dietary Fiber . . . . . . 1 g
    Sugars . . . . 9 g
Protein . . . . 25 g

Bernetha's Pork Chops

Preparation time: 20 minutes
Serves 4   Serving size: 1 chop

2	tsp sesame oil, divided
1	lb lean boneless pork chops
1	tsp minced garlic
1/2	tsp minced ginger
4	Tbsp rice wine
4	Tbsp lite soy sauce
2 1/2	Tbsp brown sugar
	Red pepper flakes (optional)
2	tsp cornstarch
2	Tbsp water

1. Heat 1 tsp oil in a skillet. Brown the pork chops, garlic, and ginger in the oil, turning once.

2. In a small bowl, combine 1 tsp oil, wine, soy sauce (omit this if you need to reduce total sodium), brown sugar, and red pepper flakes. Pour the sauce over the chops and cover tightly. Simmer over low heat until the chops are tender and cooked through, about 15–20 minutes.

3. Mix the cornstarch and water together. Remove the chops from the skillet and add the cornstarch mixture, stirring well. Cook until thickened, about 5 minutes. Pour the sauce over the chops to serve.

Exchanges
1 Carbohydrate
3 Lean Meat

Calories 257
   Calories from Fat . . 92
Total Fat . . . . 10 g
   Saturated Fat . . . . . . 4 g
Cholesterol . . . . 80 mg
Sodium . . . . 669 mg
Carbohydrate . . . . . . 12 g
   Dietary Fiber . . . . . . 0 g
   Sugars . . . . 11 g
Protein . . . . 28 g

Country-Fried Steak

Preparation time: 20 minutes
Serves 6   Serving size: 1 steak

> 1   lb lean boneless top round of beef
>
> Salt to taste (optional)
>
> Pepper to taste (optional)
>
> 1   Tbsp olive oil
>
> 2   medium onions, chopped
>
> 1   green bell pepper, seeded and chopped
>
> 1   clove garlic, chopped
>
> 2   Tbsp flour
>
> 1/2   tsp kitchen bouquet
>
> 1/2   cup water
>
> 1   cup stewed tomatoes

1. Cut the beef into 6 serving pieces. Place the pieces between sheets of waxed paper and pound with a mallet. Season the beef with salt and pepper.

2. Heat the oil in a large skillet and saute the onion, green pepper, and garlic for 5 minutes. Push to the side of the skillet and brown the beef quickly on both sides. Stir in flour and enough kitchen bouquet to make the gravy a desired color.

3. Add water and stir as the gravy thickens. Add stewed tomatoes, cover, and cook until beef is tender, about 30 minutes.

Exchanges

2 Vegetable
2 Lean Meat
1/2 Fat

Calories 178
  Calories from Fat . . 61
Total Fat . . . . 7 g
  Saturated Fat . . . . . . 3 g
Cholesterol . . . . 45 mg
Sodium . . . . 156 mg
Carbohydrate . . . . . . 11 g
  Dietary Fiber . . . . . . 1 g
  Sugars . . . . 5 g
Protein . . . . 18 g

Daddy's Favorite Pork Chops

Preparation time: 20 minutes
Serves 6   Serving size: 1 chop

6	lean pork chops
	Salt to taste (optional)
	Pepper to taste (optional)
1	medium onion, chopped
3/4	cup catsup
1	cup water
2	Tbsp Worcestershire sauce
2	Tbsp apple cider vinegar
2	Tbsp brown sugar
1 1/4	tsp paprika
1 1/4	tsp chili powder

1. Heat the oven to 325 degrees. Season the pork chops with salt and pepper (if desired) and place in a baking dish with a cover. Spread chopped onions evenly over the chops.

2. Combine the remaining ingredients in a small bowl, mix well, and pour over the chops. Cover and bake for 1 1/2 hours. Bake uncovered for the last 20 minutes.

Exchanges
1 Carbohydrate
2 Lean Meat

Calories 215
   Calories from Fat . . 59
Total Fat . . . . 7 g
   Saturated Fat . . . . . . 3 g
Cholesterol . . . . 63 mg
Sodium . . . . 460 mg
Carbohydrate . . . . . . 16 g
   Dietary Fiber . . . . . . 1 g
   Sugars . . . . 10 g
Protein . . . . 23 g

Easy Beef Casserole

Preparation time: 15 minutes
Serves 4   Serving size: 4 oz

1 lb lean, boneless top round steak, cut into bite-
sized pieces
2 cups sliced carrots
1 medium onion, chopped
1/2 cup water
2 Tbsp Worcestershire sauce
1 tsp garlic powder
1 tsp parsley
2 Tbsp red wine
1/2 tsp salt
Pepper to taste (optional)

1. Heat the oven to 350 degrees. Place the steak, carrots, and onions in a casserole dish.

2. Combine the remaining ingredients in a small bowl and mix well. Cover the dish tightly with aluminum foil and bake for 2 hours, keeping the dish covered at all times.

Exchanges
2 Vegetable
3 Lean Meat

Calories 216
   Calories from Fat . . 59
Total Fat . . . . 7 g
   Saturated Fat . . . . . . 4 g
Cholesterol . . . . 12 mg
Sodium . . . . 444 mg
Carbohydrate . . . . . . 12 g
   Dietary Fiber . . . . . . 3 g
   Sugars . . . . 5 g
Protein . . . . 26 g

Marinated Steak

Preparation time: 20 minutes
Serves 8   Serving size: 4 oz

- 2 lb lean boneless sirloin, about 3/4 inch thick
- 1 tsp salt
- 1/4 tsp pepper
- 1 Tbsp garlic powder, divided
- 1/2 cup dry red wine
- 1 tsp parsley
- 1 tsp oregano
- 1 tsp olive oil
- 1/2 cup fresh mushrooms

1. Rub the beef with salt, pepper, and garlic powder. Mix together the wine, parsley, and oregano. Pour over the meat and marinate in the refrigerator for 12 hours, turning often.

2. Remove the steak from the marinade and pat dry with a paper towel. Discard the marinade.

3. Heat the oil in a heavy skillet and saute the mushrooms on high heat, turning frequently, for 3 minutes. Add the steak and saute for 4–7 minutes on each side, depending on desired doneness.

Exchanges
3 Lean Meat

Calories 148
  Calories from Fat . . 49
Total Fat . . . . 5 g
  Saturated Fat . . . . . . 3 g
Cholesterol . . . . 64 mg
Sodium . . . . 340 mg
Carbohydrate . . . . 1 g
  Dietary Fiber . . . . . . 0 g
  Sugars . . . . 0 g
Protein . . . . 22 g

Pork Chops with Fruit Sauce

Preparation time: 15 minutes
Serves 4   Serving size: 1 chop

2	Tbsp sugar
2	Tbsp cornstarch
1/8	tsp allspice
1	cup water
1/4	cup orange juice
2	Tbsp lemon juice
1/2	cup raisins
1/4	cup flour
1/3	tsp salt
1/4	tsp pepper
1	lb lean boneless pork chops
2	tsp canola oil
4	orange slices

1. Combine the sugar, cornstarch, and allspice in a small saucepan. Add the water and cook over low heat until thick, stirring constantly. Stir in the fruit juices and raisins. Remove from heat and set aside.

2. Combine the flour, salt, and pepper. Dredge the pork chops in the flour mixture. Heat the oil in a skillet over medium-high heat, and brown the chops quickly on both sides.

3. Pour the juice mixture over the chops and cover. Reduce heat and simmer for 30 minutes or until the chops are tender. Garnish with orange slices and serve.

Exchanges
2 Fruit
4 Lean Meat

Calories	349
Calories from Fat	. . 95
Total Fat	11 g
Saturated Fat	3 g
Cholesterol	80 mg
Sodium	209 mg
Carbohydrate	34 g
Dietary Fiber	1 g
Sugars	21 g
Protein	30 g

Pork Roast

Preparation time: 20 minutes
Serves 8   Serving size: 4 oz

- 1/3 cup lite soy sauce
- 1/2 cup dry sherry
- 2 cloves garlic, minced
- 1 Tbsp dry mustard
- 1 tsp ginger
- 2 tsp thyme
- 2 lb lean boneless pork roast

1. Combine the soy sauce, sherry, garlic, and spices in a plastic locking bag and mix well. Place the pork in the bag and marinate in the refrigerator for 10–12 hours.

2. Heat the oven to 325 degrees. Remove the pork from the marinade, discard the marinade, and roast the pork for 2 hours. Let the roast rest 15 minutes before slicing.

Exchanges
3 Medium-Fat Meat
1/2 Fat

Calories	250
Calories from Fat	156
Total Fat	17 g
Saturated Fat	7 g
Cholesterol	79 mg
Sodium	163 mg
Carbohydrate	0 g
Dietary Fiber	0 g
Sugars	0 g
Protein	21 g

Pork Supper in One Pot

Preparation time: 15 minutes
Serves 4   Serving size: 4 oz

> 1 lb lean boneless pork chops
>
> 1 10 3/4-oz can condensed tomato soup
>
> 1/2 cup water
>
> 2 tsp Worcestershire sauce
>
> 1/2 tsp salt
>
> 3 medium potatoes, peeled and quartered
>
> 4 small carrots, split lengthwise and cut into 2-inch pieces

1. In a large nonstick skillet, brown the pork chops. Pour off any fat and add the remaining ingredients (omit the salt if you need to reduce total sodium).

2. Cover the chops and cook over low heat 45 minutes or until tender.

Exchanges
2 1/2 Starch
3 Lean Meat

Calories	362
Calories from Fat	. . 84
Total Fat	9 g
Saturated Fat	4 g
Cholesterol	80 mg
Sodium	831 mg
Carbohydrate	37 g
Dietary Fiber	5 g
Sugars	10 g
Protein	32 g

Pork Tenderloin in Hoisin Sauce

Preparation time: 10 minutes
Serves 6   Serving size: 4 oz

1/4 cup lite soy sauce

2 Tbsp canola oil

1 Tbsp brown sugar

1/4 cup hoisin sauce

1 1/2 lb lean boneless pork tenderloin

2 cups cooked rice

4 stalks green onion, chopped

1. Mix the soy sauce, canola oil, brown sugar, and hoisin sauce in a plastic locking bag. Add the pork and marinate in the refrigerator for at least 1 hour or overnight.

2. Heat the oven to 350 degrees. Remove the pork from the marinade and roast it for 15 minutes on each side or until done. Let the pork rest before slicing. Serve with 1/3 cup rice and garnish with green onion.

Exchanges
1 Starch
4 Very Lean Meat

Calories 232
    Calories from Fat . . 52
Total Fat . . . . 6 g
    Saturated Fat . . . . . . 0 g
Cholesterol . . . . 65 mg
Sodium . . . . 252 mg
Carbohydrate . . . . . . 18 g
    Dietary Fiber . . . . . . 1 g
    Sugars . . . . 2 g
Protein . . . . 25 g

Quick Beef Stroganoff

Preparation time: 20 minutes
Serves 8   Serving size: 1/2 cup

1 1/2	lb lean ground beef
1	Tbsp reduced-fat margarine
3/4	cup chopped onion
1/4	cup chopped green bell pepper
1/3	cup flour
1	tsp salt
1/8	tsp garlic powder
1/4	tsp pepper
1	Tbsp Worcestershire sauce
1	6-oz can tomato paste
1	10-oz can beef broth
1	cup evaporated fat-free (skim) milk

1. Brown the ground beef in a heavy skillet. Drain off the fat, remove the beef from the skillet, and set aside. Add the margarine and saute the onion and bell pepper until tender.

2. Add the remaining ingredients slowly, stirring to blend. Cover and cook over low heat for 30 minutes. Serve over hot noodles or fluffy rice.

Exchanges
1 Starch
2 Medium-Fat Meat

Calories 247
    Calories from Fat . 111
Total Fat . . . . 12 g
    Saturated Fat . . . . . . 4 g
Cholesterol . . . . 55 mg
Sodium . . . . 547 mg
Carbohydrate . . . . . . 14 g
    Dietary Fiber . . . . . . 1 g
    Sugars . . . . 5 g
Protein . . . . 19 g

Roast Beef, Jamaican-Style

Preparation time: 20 minutes
Serves 6   Serving size: 4 oz

1 medium onion, finely chopped
3 stalks green onion, finely chopped
4 garlic cloves, finely chopped
1/2 tsp salt
1 1/2 tsp pepper
2 tsp thyme
2 tsp pimiento seeds (available at West Indian markets)
2 tsp lite soy sauce
1 Tbsp peppercorns
1 1/2 lb lean boneless beef roast
1 Tbsp olive oil

1. Mix all ingredients except the beef and the oil in a small bowl. Wash and dry the beef.

2. Using a thin, sharp knife, puncture the beef on all sides. Open the puncture 1 to 1 1/2 inches deep on all sides. Using your index finger, open the puncture sites and put in the seasoning.

3. Marinate in the refrigerator 12–24 hours. Heat the oven to 300 degrees. Place the beef in a nonstick baking dish. Rub the oil on the beef and bake for 45 minutes or until done.

Exchanges
1 Vegetable
3 Lean Meat

Calories 202
   Calories from Fat . . 80
Total Fat . . . . 9 g
   Saturated Fat . . . . . . 3 g
Cholesterol . . . . 72 mg
Sodium . . . . 302 mg
Carbohydrate . . . . 4 g
   Dietary Fiber . . . . . . 1 g
   Sugars . . . . 3 g
Protein . . . . 25 g

Roniece's Jerk Pork Tenderloin

Preparation time: 10 minutes
Serves 8   Serving size: 4 oz

> 2 lb lean boneless pork tenderloin
>
> 1/2 cup lite soy sauce
>
> 2 tsp thyme
>
> 1 tsp oregano
>
> 2 Tbsp wet jerk marinade (check the gourmet aisle of your supermarket)

1. Place the soy sauce, thyme, oregano, and jerk marinade in a plastic locking bag and mix well. Put the pork in the bag and marinate in the refrigerator for several hours.

2. Remove the pork from the bag and discard the marinade. Grill outside until the pork is well done. To achieve the best results, place the meat away from the hot coals and allow the heat to smoke the pork tenderloin. You may also broil the pork. Slice in 1/2-inch slices when done.

Exchanges
4 Very Lean Meat

Calories 138
  Calories from Fat . . 37
Total Fat . . . . 4 g
  Saturated Fat . . . . . . 0 g
Cholesterol . . . . 65 mg
Sodium . . . . 225 mg
Carbohydrate . . . . 1 g
  Dietary Fiber . . . . . . 0 g
  Sugars . . . . 1 g
Protein . . . . 24 g

Smothered Pork Chops

Preparation time: 20 minutes
Serves 6   Serving size: 4 oz

> 2 Tbsp flour
> 1/2 tsp Cajun seasoning
> Salt to taste (optional)
> Pepper to taste (optional)
> 1 1/2 lb lean boneless pork chops
> 2 Tbsp canola oil
> 1 10-oz bag frozen onion
> 1 clove garlic, minced
> 1 10-oz bag frozen green bell pepper
> 1 10-oz bag frozen celery
> 1 15-oz can stewed tomatoes
> 2 bay leaves
> 1/2 cup water
> 1/2 tsp oregano
> 1/2 tsp thyme

1. Mix the flour with the Cajun seasoning, salt, and pepper in a plastic locking bag. Add the pork chops and toss to coat.

2. Heat the oil in a large skillet and brown the chops on both sides. Remove the chops from the skillet and saute the onion, garlic, bell pepper, and celery for 10 minutes.

3. Add the remaining ingredients to the skillet and mix well. Return the pork chops to the skillet and simmer until tender.

Exchanges
1 Starch
4 Lean Meat

Calories 299
  Calories from Fat . 117
Total Fat . . . . 13 g
  Saturated Fat . . . . . . 3 g
Cholesterol . . . . 80 mg
Sodium . . . . 371 mg
Carbohydrate . . . . . . 16 g
  Dietary Fiber . . . . . . 2 g
  Sugars . . . . 6 g
Protein . . . . 30 g

Stew Beef with Vegetables

Preparation time: 20 minutes
Serves 8   Serving size: 4 oz

  2 lb lean stew beef, diced
  1 10-oz can low-fat cream of mushroom soup
  2 cups chopped onions
  2 cups sliced carrots
  1 cup chopped green bell pepper
  2 reduced-sodium beef bouillon cubes
1/2 cup red wine
  2 cups water
  4 cups cooked rice

1. Combine all ingredients except the rice in a large soup pot. Bring to a boil and reduce the heat.

2. Simmer until the beef becomes tender, about 1 to 1 1/2 hours. Add more water if necessary. Serve over 1/2 cup of hot rice.

Exchanges

2 Starch	2 Lean Meat
2 Vegetable	

Calories	313
Calories from Fat	43
Total Fat	5 g
Saturated Fat	0 g
Cholesterol	64 mg
Sodium	485 mg
Carbohydrate	35 g
Dietary Fiber	2 g
Sugars	5 g
Protein	30 g

Vegetable Beef Skillet

Preparation time: 15 minutes
Serves 6   Serving size: 1 cup

1/2 lb lean ground beef
1 large onion, sliced
1 cup frozen lima beans, thawed
1 cup frozen green beans, thawed
1 cup frozen corn kernels, thawed
1 tsp garlic salt
1/2 tsp pepper
4 medium tomatoes, peeled and cubed

1. Brown the ground beef in a large skillet, stirring to crumble. Drain off any fat. Add all ingredients except the tomatoes.

2. Cover and cook over low heat for 20 minutes. Add the tomatoes and cook for 5–10 minutes more. Serve over steamed rice or noodles.

Exchanges
1/2 Starch
2 Vegetable
1 Medium-Fat Meat

Calories 162
   Calories from Fat . . 52
Total Fat . . . . 6 g
   Saturated Fat . . . . . . 2 g
Cholesterol . . . . 24 mg
Sodium . . . . 242 mg
Carbohydrate . . . . . . 19 g
   Dietary Fiber . . . . . . 4 g
   Sugars . . . . 6 g
Protein . . . . 11 g

Willa's Lasagna

Preparation time: 30 minutes
Serves 10   Serving size: 2 × 2-inch square

- 2 tsp canola oil
- 1 clove garlic, minced
- 2 medium onions, chopped
- 3/4 cup chopped celery
- 1 green bell pepper, seeded and chopped
- 1 lb lean ground beef
- 1 6-oz can tomato paste
- 1/2 cup water
- 1/2 cup chopped tomatoes
- 4 tsp oregano
- 2 tsp basil
- 1/2 tsp salt
- 1/2 tsp pepper
- 1 16-oz pkg lasagna noodles, cooked and drained
- 2 cups reduced-fat cottage cheese
- 2 cups reduced-fat mozzarella cheese

1. Heat the oil in a large skillet and saute the garlic, onion, celery, bell pepper, and meat. Drain off any fat. Add the tomato paste, water, tomatoes, and seasonings.

2. Simmer for 2–3 hours. Heat the oven to 350 degrees. In a large baking dish, make a layer of noodles, cottage cheese, sauce, and mozzarella cheese. Repeat to make two layers. Bake for 45 minutes.

Exchanges

3 Starch
3 Lean Meat

Calories 394
   Calories from Fat . 100
Total Fat . . . . 11 g
   Saturated Fat . . . . . . 5 g
Cholesterol . . . . 44 mg
Sodium . . . . 494 mg
Carbohydrate . . . . . . 44 g
   Dietary Fiber . . . . . . 3 g
   Sugars . . . . 6 g
Protein . . . . 28 g

*M*ama's Favorite Chicken

Asian Lemon Chicken

Preparation time: 20 minutes
Serves 4   Serving size: 3–4 oz

- 2 lemons
- 2 Tbsp canola oil
- 4 boneless, skinless chicken breast halves, cut into strips
- 1/2 tsp salt
- 1/8 tsp pepper
- 1 cup sliced mushrooms
- 1/2 green bell pepper, seeded and cut into 1/4-inch strips
- 1/2 red bell pepper, seeded and cut into 1/4-inch strips
- 1/2 cup sliced green onion
- 1/2 tsp grated gingerroot
- 1/2 cup reduced-sodium, reduced-fat chicken broth
- 2 Tbsp dry sherry
- 2 Tbsp lite soy sauce
- 2 tsp cornstarch
- 1 1/2 tsp sugar

1. Peel 1 lemon; cut the rind into 1/8-inch pieces. Set aside 2 Tbsp of rind. Squeeze both lemons to yield 3 Tbsp of juice; set aside.

2. Pour the oil around the top of a wok or large skillet. Heat the oil for 2 minutes. Sprinkle the chicken with salt (omit this if you need to reduce total sodium) and pepper and add it to the wok or skillet. Stir-fry for 2 minutes. Remove the chicken and keep it warm. Add the mushrooms, 2 Tbsp lemon rind, bell pepper, green onion, and gingerroot. Stir-fry for 1 minute.

3. Combine 3 Tbsp of lemon juice, chicken broth, sherry, soy sauce, cornstarch, and sugar in a small bowl and mix well. Add the mixture to the wok and stir-fry 3 minutes or until the mixture is thickened. Return the chicken to the wok and stir-fry 1 minute. Serve with steamed rice.

Exchanges
1/2 Carbohydrate
4 Lean Meat

Calories 248
Calories from Fat . . .92
Total Fat . . . . 10 g
Saturated Fat . . . . . . 0 g
Cholesterol . . . . 72 mg
Sodium . . . . 740 mg
Carbohydrate . . . . . . 10 g
Dietary Fiber . . . . . . 2 g
Sugars . . . . 5 g
Protein . . . . 28 g

Chicken and Dumplings

Preparation time: 25 minutes
Serves 8   Serving size: 1/8 recipe

> 3 lb chicken fryer, skin removed
> 1 medium onion, chopped
> 2 garlic cloves, chopped
> 2 celery stalks, chopped
> 4 medium carrots
> 1 bay leaf
> 1 reduced-sodium chicken bouillon cube
> 1/2 tsp salt, divided
> 1/4 tsp pepper
> 3 cups flour
> 1/4 cup egg substitute

1. Cut the chicken into pieces, rinse them, and place in a large pot. Cover with water and add the vegetables and bouillon cube. Cook for 1 hour or until tender. Stir in 1/4 tsp salt and the pepper. Remove 1 cup of broth and let cool.

2. Place the flour and remaining 1/4 tsp salt in a mixing bowl. Pour the egg substitute and reserved chicken broth in the center of the bowl. Mix until a soft dough is formed. Roll the dough on a floured surface until thin. Cut the dough into strips and let it stand for 10 minutes.

3. Meanwhile, debone the chicken and bring the broth to a boil. Then drop the strips of dough into the broth. Add the chicken and continue to cook for an additional 15 minutes.

Exchanges
3 Starch
2 Very Lean Meat

Calories 311
  Calories from Fat . . 40
Total Fat . . . . 4 g
  Saturated Fat . . . . . . 2 g
Cholesterol . . . . 47 mg
Sodium . . . . 318 mg
Carbohydrate . . . . . . 44 g
  Dietary Fiber . . . . . . 3 g
  Sugars . . . . 4 g
Protein . . . . 22 g

Chicken Fricassee with Rice

Preparation time: 20 minutes
Serves 8   Serving size: 1/8 recipe

3	lb chicken fryer, skin removed
3/4	cup flour
2	tsp garlic powder
2	Tbsp chili powder
1	tsp thyme
1	tsp oregano
1/2	tsp salt
1/2	tsp pepper
3	Tbsp canola oil
1	medium onion, chopped
1	cup green bell pepper, seeded and chopped
1	cup uncooked rice
1	cup canned tomatoes, undrained
2 1/2	cups boiling water

1. Cut chicken into serving pieces, rinse, and pat dry. In a small bowl, combine the flour, garlic powder, chili powder, thyme, oregano, salt, and pepper. Dredge each chicken piece in the seasoned flour.

2. Heat the oil in a large soup pot. Set the water to boil in a separate pot. Brown the chicken on both sides. Add the onion and bell pepper and stir.

3. Add the rice, tomatoes, and water. Cover and cook until the rice is done.

Exchanges
2 Starch
2 Lean Meat
1/2 Monounsaturated Fat

Calories 304
    Calories from Fat . . 90
Total Fat . . . . 10 g
    Saturated Fat . . . . . . 2 g
Cholesterol . . . . 48 mg
Sodium . . . . 258 mg
Carbohydrate . . . . . . 33 g
    Dietary Fiber . . . . . . 2 g
    Sugars . . . . 3 g
Protein . . . . 20 g

Chicken Spaghetti

Preparation time: 35 minutes
Serves 6   Serving size: 1 cup

1/4	cup canola oil, divided
1	green bell pepper, seeded and chopped
1	cup diced celery
2	large onions, chopped
3	cloves garlic, chopped
1	16-oz can tomato puree
2	6-oz cans tomato paste
4	cups water
3	large boneless, skinless chicken breast halves, cut into pieces
1	tsp cinnamon
1/2	tsp salt
1/2	tsp pepper
1/2	tsp allspice
8	oz uncooked spaghetti

1. Heat 2 Tbsp oil in a large soup pot. Saute the green pepper, celery, onions, and garlic in the oil until tender. Add the tomato puree, paste, and water. Simmer uncovered for 1 1/2 hours. Stir often.

2. In a separate skillet, brown the chicken pieces in the remaining 2 Tbsp oil. Add the chicken, cinnamon, salt, pepper, and allspice to the sauce. Continue to simmer, covered, for 1 1/2 hours more or until the chicken is tender.

3. Cook the spaghetti according to package directions, omitting the salt, and drain. Place in a serving dish. Pour the chicken sauce over the spaghetti and serve.

Exchanges
4 Starch
2 Lean Meat

Calories 424
    Calories from Fat . 111
Total Fat . . . . 12 g
    Saturated Fat . . . . . . 0 g
Cholesterol . . . . 36 mg
Sodium . . . . 427 mg
Carbohydrate . . . . . . 58 g
    Dietary Fiber . . . . . . 7 g
    Sugars . . . . 13 g
Protein . . . . 23 g

Eunice's Curried Chicken

Preparation time: 20 minutes
Serves 6   Serving size: 1/6 recipe

3 lb chicken fryer, skin removed

1 tsp salt

2 tsp chives

3 tsp thyme

1 Tbsp canola oil

1 medium onion, chopped

2 cloves garlic, minced

1 Tbsp curry powder

1/2 cup water

1 medium apple, peeled and diced

1. Cut the chicken into pieces, rinse, and pat dry. Combine the salt, chives, and thyme in a small bowl. Roll the chicken in the seasoning.

2. Heat the oil in a large saucepan. Add the chicken pieces and brown for 5 minutes on each side. Add the onion and garlic and cook for 20 minutes.

3. Mix the curry powder with the water and add it to the chicken. Stir in the apple and enough water to cover the chicken, and cook until the chicken is tender, about 20 minutes.

Exchanges
1/2 Carbohydrate
3 Very Lean Meat
1 Fat

Calories 182
  Calories from Fat . . 70
Total Fat . . . . 8 g
  Saturated Fat . . . . . . 3 g
Cholesterol . . . . 63 mg
Sodium . . . . 449 mg
Carbohydrate . . . . 6 g
  Dietary Fiber . . . . . . 1 g
  Sugars . . . . 5 g
Protein . . . . 21 g

Honey-Mustard Chicken

Preparation time: 20 minutes
Serves 4   Serving size: 4 oz

> 1/4 cup lemon juice
>
> 2 Tbsp Dijon mustard
>
> 2 Tbsp honey
>
> 1 tsp ginger
>
> 1 tsp rosemary
>
> 2 lb chicken thighs, skin removed
>
> 1/2 cup dried breadcrumbs

1. Combine the lemon juice, mustard, honey, ginger, and rosemary in a small bowl. Place the chicken between sheets of waxed paper and pound to equal thickness.

2. Pour 1/2 of the honey-mustard sauce over the chicken. Cover and refrigerate for 20 minutes.

3. Set the oven to broil. Sprinkle the breadcrumbs over the top of the chicken and broil for 7–8 minutes. In a saucepan, warm the rest of the sauce and serve with the chicken.

Exchanges
1 1/2 Carbohydrate
2 Lean Meat

Calories 235
   Calories from Fat . . 74
Total Fat . . . . 8 g
   Saturated Fat . . . . . . 3 g
Cholesterol . . . . 64 mg
Sodium . . . . 267 mg
Carbohydrate . . . . . . 20 g
   Dietary Fiber . . . . . . 0 g
   Sugars . . . . 10 g
Protein . . . . 21 g

Lemon-Lime Chicken

Preparation time: 15 minutes
Serves 6   Serving size: 4 oz

3 lb chicken fryer, skin removed

1/4 cup lime juice

1/4 cup lemon juice

1/3 cup dry white wine

1 clove garlic, crushed

1 tsp thyme

1 tsp salt

1/8 tsp pepper

1. Cut the chicken into pieces, rinse, and pat dry. Place the chicken in a bowl or plastic bag. Combine the remaining ingredients and pour over the chicken. Marinate 2 or more hours in the refrigerator.

2. Heat the oven to 425 degrees. Spray a baking pan with nonstick cooking spray. Arrange the chicken pieces in the pan and bake for 40 minutes or until done.

Exchanges
3 Very Lean Meat
1/2 Fat

Calories	141
Calories from Fat	49
Total Fat	5 g
Saturated Fat	3 g
Cholesterol	65 mg
Sodium	160 mg
Carbohydrate	0 g
Dietary Fiber	0 g
Sugars	0 g
Protein	31 g

Mary Alice's Chicken and Rice

Preparation time: 20 minutes
Serves 6   Serving size: 1/6 recipe

4	cups boiling water
1 1/2	lb chicken thighs, skin removed
2	cups uncooked rice
1	medium green bell pepper, seeded and quartered
1	medium onion, chopped
2	bay leaves
1/2	tsp salt
1	tsp pepper
1	tsp garlic powder

1. Add the chicken to the boiling water and cook for 20 minutes. Heat the oven to 350 degrees.

2. Stir all ingredients together, including the chicken and water, in a large baking pan. Bake for 30 minutes or until the rice is done. Remove the bay leaves to serve.

Exchanges
3 1/2 Starch
1 Very Lean Meat

Calories 312
  Calories from Fat . . 37
Total Fat . . . . 4 g
  Saturated Fat . . . . . . 1 g
Cholesterol . . . . 32 mg
Sodium . . . . 225 mg
Carbohydrate . . . . . . 53 g
  Dietary Fiber . . . . . . 1 g
  Sugars . . . . 2 g
Protein . . . . 14 g

Quick Chicken Creole

Preparation time: 20 minutes
Serves 8   Serving size: 1/8 recipe

1	Tbsp canola oil
4	medium boneless, skinless chicken breast halves, cut into strips
1	14-oz can tomatoes, undrained
1	8-oz can tomato sauce
1 1/2	cups chopped green bell pepper
1/2	cup chopped celery
1/2	cup chopped onion
2	cloves garlic, minced
1/4	tsp salt
1	Tbsp basil
1	Tbsp parsley
1/4	tsp red pepper
2 2/3	cups steamed rice

1. Heat the oil in a large skillet and saute the chicken about 5 minutes on each side.

2. Add the remaining ingredients and simmer for 20 minutes. Serve over 1/3 cup steamed rice.

Exchanges
1 Starch
1 Vegetable
2 Very Lean Meat

Calories 190
  Calories from Fat . . 32
Total Fat . . . . 4 g
  Saturated Fat . . . . . . 0 g
Cholesterol . . . . 36 mg
Sodium . . . . 373 mg
Carbohydrate . . . . . . 23 g
  Dietary Fiber . . . . . . 2 g
  Sugars . . . . 4 g
Protein . . . . 16 g

Tramaine's Oven-Fried Chicken

Preparation time: 15 minutes
Serves 6   Serving size: 1/6 recipe

3 lb chicken fryer, skin removed
1 cup fat-free (skim) milk
1 tsp thyme
1 tsp garlic powder
1 tsp onion powder
1 tsp parsley
1 tsp paprika
1 tsp pepper
1/2 tsp salt
1/8 tsp red pepper
1 cup flour

1. Cut the chicken into pieces and place them in the milk. Heat the oven to 400 degrees.

2. In a large bowl, combine all remaining ingredients. Dredge each chicken piece in the flour mixture, making sure all pieces are well coated. Discard remaining flour.

3. Place the chicken in a baking pan and spray the top of the chicken with nonstick cooking spray. Bake for 45 minutes or until the chicken juices run clear.

Exchanges
1 Starch
3 Very Lean Meat
1/2 Fat

Calories 201
   Calories from Fat . . 50
Total Fat . . . . 6 g
   Saturated Fat . . . . . . 3 g
Cholesterol . . . . 55 mg
Sodium . . . . 208 mg
Carbohydrate . . . . . . 12 g
   Dietary Fiber . . . . . . 0 g
   Sugars . . . . 2 g
Protein . . . . 24 g

Rojean's Cornish Hens

Preparation time: 20 minutes
Serves 8   Serving size: 1/2 hen

4	Cornish game hens, insides removed
1/2	tsp salt
1/2	tsp pepper
1/2	tsp garlic powder
	Dash paprika
2	Tbsp reduced-fat margarine
1	medium onion, cut in 4 sections
1	celery stalk, cut in 4 sections
3/4	tsp thyme
1	bay leaf
1	cup Madeira wine
3	tsp chicken bouillon granules
1	cup boiling water
1 1/2	Tbsp cornstarch
1	tsp sugar
1	medium onion, finely chopped

1. Wash and dry the hens and heat the oven to 425 degrees. Sprinkle the hens with seasonings and rub with margarine inside and out. Place a small piece of onion and celery in each hen. Roast uncovered for 1 hour.

2. Meanwhile, in a small bowl, combine the thyme, bay leaf, and wine; set aside. Dissolve the bouillon in the boiling water. Mix in the cornstarch and sugar. Set aside.

3. When the hens are done, remove them to a heated plate and keep them warm. Pour off 1/2 cup of the drippings into a medium saucepan. Saute the onion until soft.

4. Stir the cornstarch mixture into the saucepan and bring to a boil. Reduce the heat. Stir in the wine and simmer for 5 minutes. Strain the sauce into a gravy boat and serve with the hens.

Exchanges
1/2 Carbohydrate
4 Medium-Fat Meat
1 Fat

Calories 393	
Calories from Fat . 222	
Total Fat . . . . 25 g	
Saturated Fat . . . . . . 7 g	
Cholesterol . . . . 169 mg	
Sodium . . . . 473 mg	
Carbohydrate . . . . 8 g	
Dietary Fiber . . . . . . 1 g	
Sugars . . . . 5 g	
Protein . . . . 29 g	

Stewed Chicken

Preparation time: 20 minutes
Serves 4   Serving size: 4 oz

2 lb chicken thighs, skin removed

1 tsp salt

1 tsp pepper

1 tsp thyme

1 tsp sage

1 tsp celery seeds

1 Tbsp olive oil

1 medium onion, chopped

2 cloves garlic, chopped

1 cup flour

4 cups reduced-sodium, reduced-fat chicken broth

1. Season the chicken with the salt (omit this if you need to reduce total sodium), pepper, thyme, sage, and celery seeds.

2. Heat the oil in a large skillet. Add the onion and garlic and saute 2 minutes. Add the chicken and brown on both sides. Remove the chicken from the skillet.

3. Make a paste out of the flour and broth. Add the paste to the pan drippings. Stir until thick. Return the chicken to the skillet and mix well. Cook for 30 minutes or until the chicken is tender.

Exchanges
2 Starch
2 Medium-Fat Meat

Calories 316
    Calories from Fat . . 96
Total Fat . . . . 11 g
    Saturated Fat . . . . . . 3 g
Cholesterol . . . . 63 mg
Sodium . . . . 1186 mg
Carbohydrate . . . . . . 28 g
    Dietary Fiber . . . . . . 1 g
    Sugars . . . . 3 g
Protein . . . . 24 g

Sunshine State Chicken à la Orange

Preparation time: 20 minutes
Serves 4   Serving size: 4 oz

- 1 cup chopped tangerine or orange
- 1/4 cup pineapple juice
- 1/8 tsp ground mace
- 1/8 tsp ginger
- 1/8 tsp red pepper flakes
- 4 boneless, skinless chicken breast halves
- 1 cup orange sections
- 1/2 cup pineapple cubes
- 1/2 cup sliced strawberries

1. Place the chopped oranges, juice, and spices in a blender or food processor. Blend or process until liquified. Pour over the chicken and refrigerate for 30 minutes.

2. Heat the oven to broil. Remove the chicken from the marinade and discard the marinade. Broil or grill the chicken for 5 minutes per side or until the chicken juices run clear.

3. Meanwhile, mix the fruit together in a small bowl. Top the chicken with the fruit and serve.

Exchanges
1 Fruit
4 Very Lean Meat

Calories 185
   Calories from Fat . . 29
Total Fat . . . . 3 g
   Saturated Fat . . . . . . 0 g
Cholesterol . . . . 72 mg
Sodium . . . . 63 mg
Carbohydrate . . . . . . 11 g
   Dietary Fiber . . . . . . 2 g
   Sugars . . . . 8 g
Protein . . . . 27 g

Turkey Breakfast Sausage Patties

Preparation time: 15 minutes
Serves 12   Serving size: 2 patties

2 1/2	tsp sage
1/4	tsp salt
1	tsp pepper
3/4	tsp marjoram
1/4	tsp allspice
1/4	tsp nutmeg
1/2	tsp dry mustard
1	tsp crushed red pepper flakes
1/4	cup warm water
1 1/2	lb lean ground turkey breast

1. Mix the spices together with the warm water. Add to the meat and mix thoroughly. Refrigerate up to 12 hours to develop the flavor.

2. Shape the meat into 24 patties and fry on each side in a nonstick skillet until done, about 7–8 minutes total.

Exchanges
2 Very Lean Meat

Calories	66
Calories from Fat	12
Total Fat	1 g
Saturated Fat	0 g
Cholesterol	30 mg
Sodium	75 mg
Carbohydrate	0 g
Dietary Fiber	0 g
Sugars	0 g
Protein	13 g

Turkey Sloppy Joes

Preparation time: 20 minutes
Serves 4   Serving size: 1/2 cup

2	tsp canola oil
1	cup chopped onions
1	cup chopped green bell pepper
1	lb lean ground turkey breast
1	cup tomato sauce
1	tsp brown sugar
1/2	cup catsup
1	tsp red pepper flakes
2	tsp wine vinegar
1/4	tsp pepper

1. Heat the oil in a large skillet and saute the onion and bell pepper until translucent. Add the turkey and cook about 5 minutes. Drain off any fat.

2. Add the remaining ingredients and mix well. Simmer 15 minutes and serve on buns.

3. To reduce the sodium content of this recipe, use salt-free tomato sauce.

Exchanges
1 Starch   3 Very Lean Meat
1 Vegetable
1/2 Monounsaturated Fat

Calories	239
Calories from Fat	. . 51
Total Fat	6 g
Saturated Fat	0 g
Cholesterol	68 mg
Sodium	787 mg
Carbohydrate	21 g
Dietary Fiber	2 g
Sugars	11 g
Protein	27 g

Key Lime Pie, *p. 187*

Chicken Fricassee with Rice, *p. 55*
Southern Spiced Tea, *p. 168*

Salmon Croquette, *p. 81*

Spicy Shrimp, *p. 88*

*M*ama's Favorite Seafood

Baked Flounder au Gratin

Preparation time: 15 minutes
Serves 4   Serving size: 3 oz

> 1 large flounder (about 2 lb)
> Salt to taste (optional)
> Juice of 1 lemon
> 1/4 cup dried breadcrumbs
> 1/4 cup shredded reduced-fat cheddar cheese
> 3 Tbsp reduced-fat margarine
> 1/2 cup minced onion

1. Have your fish dealer dress the fish for you, which means removing the scales, insides, head, and tail.

2. Heat the oven to 375 degrees. Sprinkle the fish with salt and lemon juice. Lay fish in shallow nonstick baking dish.

3. Cover with breadcrumbs, cheese, small lumps of margarine, and onion. Bake for 35–45 minutes or until fish flakes easily when tested with a fork. Baste the fish from time to time with the pan juices.

Exchanges
1/2 Starch
3 Very Lean Meat
1/2 Fat

Calories 167
  Calories from Fat . . 55
Total Fat . . . . 6 g
  Saturated Fat . . . . . . 1 g
Cholesterol . . . . 48 mg
Sodium . . . . 254 mg
Carbohydrate . . . . 8 g
  Dietary Fiber . . . . . . 1 g
  Sugars . . . . 2 g
Protein . . . . 19 g

Crabmeat au Gratin

Preparation time: 15 minutes
Serves 6   Serving size: 1/2 cup

2	Tbsp reduced-fat margarine
1/2	green bell pepper, seeded and minced
1/2	medium onion, chopped
3	Tbsp flour
2	cups fat-free (skim) milk
2	cups crabmeat, flaked and shell pieces removed
1/4	tsp salt
	Dash nutmeg
1/2	cup shredded reduced-fat cheddar cheese
1/4	cup dried breadcrumbs

1. Heat the oven to 350 degrees. Melt the margarine in a large skillet and saute the bell pepper and onion for 2 minutes.

2. Add the flour, milk, crabmeat, salt, and nutmeg. Cook for 10 minutes.

3. Pour the crabmeat into a shallow nonstick baking dish. Sprinkle with shredded cheese and breadcrumbs. Bake until the cheese browns, about 20 minutes.

Exchanges
1 Starch
2 Very Lean Meat

Calories	154
Calories from Fat	. . 45
Total Fat	5 g
Saturated Fat	2 g
Cholesterol	45 mg
Sodium	390 mg
Carbohydrate	12 g
Dietary Fiber	1 g
Sugars	5 g
Protein	15 g

Crabmeat Delights

Preparation time: 20 minutes
Serves 6   Serving size: 1 ramekin

1 Tbsp reduced-fat margarine

8 mushrooms, sliced

1 Tbsp finely diced green bell pepper

1/2 cup dried breadcrumbs

2 pieces pimiento, diced

1/2 cup reduced-fat mayonnaise

1 tsp mustard

1/4 tsp salt

1/4 tsp white pepper

1 lb lump crabmeat, flaked and shell pieces removed

1. Melt the margarine in a small skillet. Saute the mushrooms and bell pepper for 4 minutes. Remove the vegetables with a slotted spoon and place in a medium bowl.

2. Turn off the heat under the skillet and mix the breadcrumbs with the margarine. Set aside. Heat the oven to 350 degrees.

3. Add the pimiento, mayonnaise, mustard, salt, and pepper to the bowl and mix well. Add the crabmeat, trying to keep large lumps together.

4. Divide the mixture into 6 ramekins. Sprinkle each ramekin with the breadcrumb mixture. Bake for 10 minutes or until lightly brown.

Exchanges
1 Starch
2 Lean Meat

Calories 179
  Calories from Fat . . 74
Total Fat . . . . 8 g
  Saturated Fat . . . . . . 1 g
Cholesterol . . . . 53 mg
Sodium . . . . 541 mg
Carbohydrate . . . . . . 11 g
  Dietary Fiber . . . . . . 1 g
  Sugars . . . . 2 g
Protein . . . . 15 g

Curtis' Favorite Shrimp

Preparation time: 20 minutes
Serves 8   Serving size: 1/2 cup

- 1/2 cup reduced-fat margarine
- 1 cup sliced fresh mushrooms
- 1 medium onion, chopped
- 2 cloves garlic, minced
- 1 8-oz can chopped tomatoes, with juice
- 1/4 cup lemon juice
- 1/4 cup chopped fresh parsley
- 1/8 tsp salt
- Pepper to taste (optional)
- 4 Tbsp tomato paste
- 1 1/2 lb shelled, deveined shrimp
- 4 cups cooked pasta, any shape

1. Melt the margarine in a large skillet and saute the mushrooms, onion, and garlic. Add the tomatoes, lemon juice, parsley, salt, and pepper. If the mixture appears thin, add enough tomato paste to thicken.

2. Simmer, uncovered, for 15 minutes. Add the shrimp the last 5 minutes. Spoon over pasta and serve hot.

Exchanges

1 Starch	2 Lean Meat
1 Vegetable	

Calories 230
    Calories from Fat . . 56
Total Fat . . . . 6 g
    Saturated Fat . . . . . . 1 g
Cholesterol . . . . 119 mg
Sodium . . . . 316 mg
Carbohydrate . . . . . . 25 g
    Dietary Fiber . . . . . . 2 g
    Sugars . . . . 3 g
Protein . . . . 17 g

Daughn's Jerk Fish

Preparation time: 20 minutes
Serves 4   Serving size: 4 oz

> 4 whole medium-sized fish (snapper or trout), dressed
>
> 1 small onion, finely chopped
>
> 6 cloves garlic, finely chopped
>
> 2 tsp ground pimiento seeds (available in West Indian markets)
>
> 2 Tbsp thyme
>
> 1/3–1/2 cup jerk sauce (check the gourmet aisle of your supermarket)
>
> 2 Tbsp lite soy sauce
>
> 2 tsp olive oil

1. Make 2 diagonal cuts on either side of each fish. Combine the onion, garlic, ground pimiento seeds, and thyme in a small bowl. Combine the jerk sauce, soy sauce, and olive oil in a shallow dish.

2. Place the bowl seasonings inside the fish. Place the fish in the shallow dish, cover, and marinate overnight or 4–6 hours before baking.

3. Heat the oven to 300 degrees. Wrap each fish individually in foil and bake for 30 minutes.

Exchanges
1/2 Carbohydrate
4 Very Lean Meat

Calories 186
  Calories from Fat . . 25
Total Fat . . . . 3 g
  Saturated Fat . . . . . . 0 g
Cholesterol . . . . 52 mg
Sodium . . . . 458 mg
Carbohydrate . . . . 8 g
  Dietary Fiber . . . . . . 1 g
  Sugars . . . . 6 g
Protein . . . . 30 g

Devona's Crab Cakes

Preparation time: 20 minutes
Serves 6   Serving size: 1 crab cake

2 cups crabmeat, flaked and shell pieces removed

1 cup dried breadcrumbs

1 cup egg substitute

1/2 cup evaporated fat-free (skim) milk

1/2 tsp salt

1/8 tsp dry mustard

1 Tbsp grated onion

1 tsp parsley

1 tsp Worcestershire sauce

1. In a small bowl, mix the crabmeat and breadcrumbs together.

2. In a separate bowl, combine the egg substitute and evaporated milk and mix well. Add the crabmeat mixture to the egg and milk mixture.

3. Stir in the salt, mustard, onion, parsley, and Worcestershire sauce. Heat the oven to broil and shape the mixture into 6 patties. Broil the crab cakes, turning once, until brown, for a total of 7–8 minutes.

Exchanges
1 Starch
2 Very Lean Meat

Calories 146
   Calories from Fat . . 14
Total Fat . . . . 2 g
   Saturated Fat . . . . . . 0 g
Cholesterol . . . . 34 mg
Sodium . . . . 546 mg
Carbohydrate . . . . . . 17 g
   Dietary Fiber . . . . . . 0 g
   Sugars . . . . 4 g
Protein . . . . 15 g

Grilled Catfish

Preparation time: 20 minutes
Serves 6   Serving size: 1 fish

6 medium whole catfish, dressed

1/3 cup olive oil

Juice of 6 lemons

1 tsp Dijon mustard

2 Tbsp Worcestershire sauce

1/2 tsp salt

1 tsp paprika

1. Heat an outside grill or set the oven to broil. Combine all ingredients except the fish in a small bowl.

2. Place the fish on the grill or broiler and cook for 20 minutes on each side, basting frequently with the sauce.

Exchanges
4 Lean Meat
1 Monounsaturated Fat

Calories 278
    Calories from Fat . . 159
Total Fat . . . . 18 g
    Saturated Fat . . . . . . 6 g
Cholesterol . . . . 91 mg
Sodium . . . . 247 mg
Carbohydrate . . . . 2 g
    Dietary Fiber . . . . . . 0 g
    Sugars . . . . 1 g
Protein . . . . 27 g

Oven-Fried Fish

Preparation time: 15 minutes
Serves 8   Serving size: 4 oz

2 lb dressed fish, cut into bite-sized pieces

1 tsp salt

1 cup fat-free (skim) milk

1 cup dried breadcrumbs

1 tsp basil

1 tsp oregano

2 Tbsp melted reduced-fat margarine

1. Heat the oven to 500 degrees. In a shallow dish, mix the salt and the milk.

2. In a separate bowl, combine the breadcrumbs, basil, and oregano. Dip the fish pieces in the milk and then roll them in the breadcrumb mixture.

3. Place the fish in a nonstick baking dish. Pour the melted butter over the fish and bake 10–12 minutes or until the fish flakes easily when tested with a fork. Serve immediately.

Exchanges
1 Starch
3 Very Lean Meat

Calories 186
    Calories from Fat . . 31
Total Fat . . . . 3 g
    Saturated Fat . . . . . . 0 g
Cholesterol . . . . 41 mg
Sodium . . . . 494 mg
Carbohydrate . . . . . . 12 g
    Dietary Fiber . . . . . . 0 g
    Sugars . . . . 2 g
Protein . . . . 26 g

Quick Tuna Casserole

Preparation time: 20 minutes
Serves 6   Serving size: 1 cup

1   5-oz pkg wide egg noodles

3   cups boiling water

1   10-oz can condensed low-fat mushroom soup

1/3   cup fat-free (skim) milk

1   6 1/2-oz can water-packed tuna

1   cup frozen green peas

1   cup dried breadcrumbs

1. Cook the noodles in the boiling water about 2 minutes. Cover, remove from heat, and let stand about 10 minutes. Heat the oven to 350 degrees.

2. Meanwhile, combine the mushroom soup, milk, tuna, and peas in a medium bowl. Rinse the noodles with warm water and drain well. Fold the noodles into the tuna mixture and pour into a nonstick 1-quart casserole.

3. Sprinkle the casserole with breadcrumbs and bake for 30 minutes.

Exchanges
2 1/2 Starch
1 Very Lean Meat

Calories 248
    Calories from Fat . . 33
Total Fat . . . . 4 g
    Saturated Fat . . . . . . 0 g
Cholesterol . . . . 33 mg
Sodium . . . . 681 mg
Carbohydrate . . . . . . 38 g
    Dietary Fiber . . . . . . 3 g
    Sugars . . . . 4 g
Protein . . . . 16 g

Rogelle's Shrimp Creole

Preparation time: 20 minutes
Serves 8   Serving size: 1 cup

2 Tbsp corn oil
1 1/2 cups chopped onion
2 tsp minced garlic
Chopped hot chili pepper (as tolerated)
1 cup chopped celery
5 medium tomatoes, peeled, seeded, and chopped
Salt to taste (optional)
Pepper to taste (optional)
1 Tbsp lime juice
2 bay leaves
1 Tbsp parsley
1 tsp Worcestershire sauce
2 lb peeled and deveined shrimp

1. Heat the oil in a large skillet. Add the onion, garlic, chili pepper, and celery and saute until the onion is tender. Do not brown.

2. Add the tomatoes, salt, pepper, lime juice, bay leaves, and parsley. Simmer, uncovered, until the sauce is slightly reduced. Remove the bay leaves.

3. Add the Worcestershire sauce and shrimp and cook until the shrimp is done, about 10 minutes. Do not overcook. Serve with hot rice.

Exchanges
2 Vegetable
2 Very Lean Meat
1/2 Polyunsaturated Fat

Calories 152
  Calories from Fat . . 42
Total Fat . . . . 5 g
  Saturated Fat . . . . . . 1 g
Cholesterol . . . . 161 mg
Sodium . . . . 215 mg
Carbohydrate . . . . 9 g
  Dietary Fiber . . . . . . 2 g
  Sugars . . . . 5 g
Protein . . . . 19 g

Salmon Croquette

Preparation time: 15 minutes
Serves 4   Serving size: 1 patty

  1 15 1/2-oz can red salmon, drained
  1 medium onion, diced
1/2 medium green bell pepper, diced
  1 Tbsp chopped fresh parsley
1/2 Tbsp lemon juice
1/4 cup egg substitute
  3 slices whole-wheat bread, crumbled
1/4 tsp pepper
  2 Tbsp canola oil

1. In a medium bowl, break the salmon into small pieces with a fork. Remove the bones and skin.

2. Add the onion, bell pepper, parsley, lemon juice, egg substitute, bread, and pepper. Form the mixture into 4 patties.

3. Heat the oil in a medium skillet and cook the patties over medium heat. Brown for 3 minutes on each side and serve.

Exchanges

1 Starch   3 Lean Meat
1/2 Monounsaturated Fat

Calories 271
  Calories from Fat . 122
Total Fat . . . . 14 g
  Saturated Fat . . . . . . 0 g
Cholesterol . . . . 52 mg
Sodium . . . . 651 mg
Carbohydrate . . . . . . 15 g
  Dietary Fiber . . . . . . 2 g
  Sugars . . . . 4 g
Protein . . . . 22 g

Salmon with Lime Sauce

Preparation time: 20 minutes
Serves 6   Serving size: 4 oz

1 1/2 lb raw salmon fillets
1/2 cup flour
1/4 tsp salt
1/2 tsp pepper
2 Tbsp corn oil
1 cup water
2 cups reduced-sodium, reduced-fat chicken broth
3 Tbsp lime juice
1 Tbsp capers

1. Cut the salmon into 6 pieces and place them in a plastic bag. Add the flour, salt, and pepper and shake to coat well.

2. Heat the oil in a large skillet. Brown the salmon pieces lightly for 2 minutes on each side.

3. Remove the salmon pieces from the skillet and place them on a plate. Add the water, chicken broth, lime juice, and capers to the skillet and bring the mixture to a boil. Stir well and add the salmon back to the skillet.

4. Reduce the heat and cook the salmon until done, about 5–10 minutes. Serve with a hot baked potato and a salad.

Exchanges
1/2 Starch
3 Lean Meat
1 Fat

Calories 252
  Calories from Fat . 118
Total Fat . . . . 13 g
  Saturated Fat . . . . . . 4 g
Cholesterol . . . . 68 mg
Sodium . . . . 392 mg
Carbohydrate . . . . . . 9 g
  Dietary Fiber . . . . . . 0 g
  Sugars . . . . 0 g
Protein . . . . 23 g

Seafood Creole

Preparation time: 20 minutes
Serves 8   Serving size: 1 cup

1/4	cup corn oil
1/4	cup flour
1	cup hot water
1	lb boneless fish, cut into pieces
1	16-oz can tomato sauce
1/2	cup chopped green onion
1/4	cup chopped green bell pepper
4	cloves garlic, minced
1/4	tsp salt
1	tsp thyme
2	bay leaves
1/4	cup chopped fresh parsley
	Dash cayenne pepper

1. Heat the oil in a large skillet and blend in the flour. Stir constantly until flour browns. Be careful not to scorch the roux.

2. Add the water gradually, and cook until thick and smooth.

3. Add the remaining ingredients, stir well, and simmer for 15 minutes. Remove the bay leaves before serving over hot rice.

Exchanges
1/2 Starch
2 Very Lean Meat
1 Polyunsaturated Fat

Calories 161
 Calories from Fat . . 73
Total Fat . . . . 8 g
 Saturated Fat . . . . . . 2 g
Cholesterol . . . . 18 mg
Sodium . . . . 474 mg
Carbohydrate . . . . 9 g
 Dietary Fiber . . . . . . 1 g
 Sugars . . . . 4 g
Protein . . . . 13 g

Shrimp and Pasta

Preparation time: 20 minutes
Serves 10   Serving size: 1 cup

16	oz uncooked linguini noodles
1 1/2	lb cooked, peeled, deveined shrimp
6	oz frozen snow peas, thawed
5	medium tomatoes, chopped
1/3	cup olive oil
1/3	cup wine vinegar
1/4	cup chopped fresh parsley
1	tsp oregano
1/2	tsp garlic powder
1/2	tsp pepper

1. Cook the linguini according to package directions, omitting the salt, and drain. Rinse with cold water and drain again.

2. Place the linguini, shrimp, snow peas, and tomatoes in a large bowl. In a separate bowl, whisk the remaining ingredients together and pour over the pasta. Toss gently to mix. Cover and chill for 2 hours. Serve with warm, crusty bread.

Exchanges
2 1/2 Starch
2 Very Lean Meat
1 Monounsaturated Fat

Calories 326
  Calories from Fat . . 81
Total Fat . . . . 9 g
  Saturated Fat . . . . . . 2 g
Cholesterol . . . . 132 mg
Sodium . . . . 163 mg
Carbohydrate . . . . . . 39 g
  Dietary Fiber . . . . . . 2 g
  Sugars . . . . 5 g
Protein . . . . 21 g

Shrimp and Rice

Preparation time: 20 minutes
Serves 8   Serving size: 1/2 cup

> 1 Tbsp canola oil
> 1 medium onion, chopped
> 1 medium green bell pepper, chopped
> 1 1/2 lb cooked, peeled shrimp, chopped
> 8 oz tomato sauce
> 4 cups water
> 1/2 tsp thyme
> 2 bay leaves
> 1/2 tsp salt
> 1/2 tsp garlic powder
> 2 cups uncooked rice

1. Heat the oil in a large saucepan and saute the onion and bell pepper until slightly tender. Add the shrimp, tomato sauce, water, thyme, bay leaves, and seasonings. Simmer 3 minutes.

2. Add the rice, stir well, and simmer on low heat for 20 minutes.

Exchanges
2 1/2 Starch
1 Vegetable
2 Very Lean Meat

Calories 290
   Calories from Fat . . 28
Total Fat . . . . 3 g
   Saturated Fat . . . . . . 0 g
Cholesterol . . . . 165 mg
Sodium . . . . 522 mg
Carbohydrate . . . . . . 42 g
   Dietary Fiber . . . . . . 1 g
   Sugars . . . . 3 g
Protein . . . . 22 g

Shrimp Fried Rice

Preparation time: 20 minutes
Serves 8   Serving size: 1 cup

2 tsp sesame oil

1 cup chopped green onion

1/2 cup chopped green bell pepper

1/2 cup chopped celery

1 cup sliced mushrooms

1 1/2 lb peeled and deveined shrimp

3 cups cooked rice

1/2 cup bean sprouts

1/8 tsp salt

1 tsp pepper

1 tsp garlic powder

2 Tbsp lite soy sauce

1 cup egg substitute

1. Heat the oil in a large wok or skillet. Stir-fry the onion, bell pepper, celery, and mushrooms for 5 minutes. Add the shrimp and stir-fry until pink.

2. Add the rice, bean sprouts, salt, pepper, garlic powder, and soy sauce. Stir-fry for 10 minutes.

3. Make a hole in the middle of the mixture and pour in the egg substitute. Cook the egg until done and mix into rice mixture. Serve hot.

Exchanges
1 1/2 Starch
2 Very Lean Meat

Calories 206
    Calories from Fat . . 21
Total Fat . . . . 2 g
    Saturated Fat . . . . . . 0 g
Cholesterol . . . . . . 129 mg
Sodium . . . . 379 mg
Carbohydrate . . . . . . 22 g
    Dietary Fiber . . . . . . 1 g
    Sugars . . . . 3 g
Protein . . . . 23 g

Shrimp Jambalaya

Preparation time: 20 minutes
Serves 8   Serving size: 3/4 cup

2	Tbsp olive oil
1 1/2	lb peeled and deveined shrimp
1	medium onion, chopped
1	medium green bell pepper, chopped
2	cups cooked rice
1	16-oz can tomato sauce
1	tsp Cajun seasoning
	Salt to taste (optional)
	Pepper to taste (optional)
	Hot pepper sauce to taste (optional)

1. Heat the oil in a large skillet and saute the shrimp, onion, and bell pepper until the shrimp is pink.

2. Stir in the remaining ingredients and cook until heated through.

Exchanges
1 Starch
1 Vegetable
2 Very Lean Meat
1/2 Monounsaturated Fat

Calories 203
  Calories from Fat . . 32
Total Fat . . . . 4 g
  Saturated Fat . . . . . . 1 g
Cholesterol . . . . 129 mg
Sodium . . . . 626 mg
Carbohydrate . . . . . . 19 g
  Dietary Fiber . . . . . . 1 g
  Sugars . . . . 5 g
Protein . . . . 20 g

Spicy Shrimp

Preparation time: 20 minutes
Serves 6   Serving size: 1/2 cup

1 1/2	lb uncooked, peeled, and deveined shrimp
1	Tbsp rum
1/4	cup vinegar
2	Tbsp lite soy sauce
4	tsp sugar
2	tsp cornstarch
2	Tbsp sesame oil
3	cloves garlic, minced
1/4	tsp red pepper flakes
1/2	cup bamboo shoots
2	stalks green onion, thinly sliced
1 1/2	Tbsp minced fresh ginger
2	stalks celery, cut into 1/2-inch slices

1. In a medium bowl, toss the shrimp with the rum. In a separate bowl, combine the vinegar, soy sauce, sugar, and cornstarch.

2. Heat the oil in a large wok or skillet and stir-fry the garlic, red pepper flakes, bamboo shoots, onion, ginger, and celery for 3 minutes.

3. Add the shrimp and stir-fry just until the shrimp turns pink. Add the sauce and cook until the sauce bubbles and thickens. Serve with steamed rice.

Exchanges
1 Vegetable
2 Lean Meat

Calories 143
    Calories from Fat . . 49
Total Fat . . . . 5 g
    Saturated Fat . . . . . . 1 g
Cholesterol . . . . 160 mg
Sodium . . . . 398 mg
Carbohydrate . . . . 4 g
    Dietary Fiber . . . . . . 1 g
    Sugars . . . . 3 g
Protein . . . . 18 g

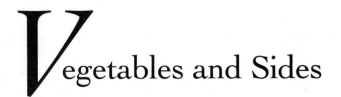

Vegetables and Sides

Baked Acorn Squash

Preparation time: 10 minutes
Serves 4   Serving size: 1/4 squash

    1 medium acorn squash

    2 tsp honey

  1/4 tsp nutmeg

  1/4 tsp cinnamon

  1/4 tsp cloves

    1 Tbsp reduced-fat margarine

1. Heat the oven to 350 degrees. Cut the squash lengthwise and remove the seeds and fibers. Place the squash in a baking dish and cover with 1/2 inch of water.

2. Sprinkle with honey and spices and dot with margarine. Bake, covered, for 30 minutes. Uncover for the last 10 minutes of cooking to brown. The squash should be tender when touched with a fork.

Exchanges
1/2 Starch
1/2 Fat

Calories 51
   Calories from Fat . . 17
Total Fat . . . . 2 g
   Saturated Fat . . . . . . 0 g
Cholesterol . . . . 0 mg
Sodium . . . . 25 mg
Carbohydrate . . . . 9 g
   Dietary Fiber . . . . . . 2 g
   Sugars . . . . 5 g
Protein . . . . 1 g

Boiled Rutabagas

Preparation time: 15 minutes
Serves 6   Serving size: 1/2 cup

2 large rutabagas

1 medium onion, chopped

3 oz smoked turkey breast

1. Peel the rutabagas and chop into cubes. Place the rutabagas in a large saucepan and add the onion and turkey. Fill the pan halfway with water.

2. Bring to a boil and then reduce heat. Cover and simmer until the rutabagas are tender, about 30–45 minutes.

Exchanges

1 Starch

Calories 88
   Calories from Fat . . . 5
Total Fat . . . . 1 g
   Saturated Fat . . . . . . 0 g
Cholesterol . . . . 7 mg
Sodium . . . . 205 mg
Carbohydrate . . . . . . 17 g
   Dietary Fiber . . . . . . 3 g
   Sugars . . . . 11 g
Protein . . . . 5 g

Broccoli Casserole

Preparation time: 15 minutes
Serves 12   Serving size: 1/2 cup

 2   12-oz pkg frozen chopped broccoli, defrosted
1/2 cup egg substitute
 1   10-oz can low-fat cream of celery soup
 1   medium onion, finely chopped
 1   Tbsp chopped garlic
1/4 tsp pepper
 2   tsp reduced-fat margarine
 1   8-oz pkg stuffing mix
 4   oz shredded reduced-fat cheddar cheese

1. Heat the oven to 350 degrees. Spray a baking dish with nonstick cooking spray and place the broccoli in the dish. Mix the egg, soup, onion, garlic, and pepper together and pour over the broccoli.

2. Melt the margarine and stir it into the stuffing mix. Pour the stuffing over the broccoli, spread evenly, and sprinkle the cheese on top. Bake for 35 minutes. Let stand 10 minutes before serving.

Exchanges
1 Starch
1 Vegetable
1 Saturated Fat

Calories 150
 Calories from Fat . . 35
Total Fat . . . . 4 g
 Saturated Fat . . . . . . 2 g
Cholesterol . . . . 8 mg
Sodium . . . . 560 mg
Carbohydrate . . . . . . 21 g
 Dietary Fiber . . . . . . 3 g
 Sugars . . . . 3 g
Protein . . . . 8 g

Butter Beans with Smoked Turkey

Preparation time: 10 minutes
Serves 8   Serving size: 1 cup

8	oz smoked turkey breast
1/4	cup chopped onion
1	lb dried butter beans (mature lima beans), soaked overnight
1	clove garlic, minced
1/8	tsp pepper
1	bay leaf
1	tsp thyme
1/4	tsp salt

1. Boil the turkey and onion in 1 quart of water for 45 minutes.

2. Place the beans, garlic, pepper, bay leaf, and thyme in the water and cook for 1 hour or until the beans are tender. Add the salt in the final 15 minutes of cooking to prevent the beans from becoming tough.

Exchanges
2 1/2 Starch
1 Very Lean Meat

Calories 216
    Calories from Fat . . . 6
Total Fat . . . . 1 g
    Saturated Fat . . . . . . 0 g
Cholesterol . . . . 13 mg
Sodium . . . . 423 mg
Carbohydrate . . . . . . 36 g
    Dietary Fiber . . . . . 11 g
    Sugars . . . . 5 g
Protein . . . . 18 g

Cabbage Casserole

Preparation time: 20 minutes
Serves 8   Serving size: 1 cup

> 1 lb lean ground beef
> 1 medium onion, chopped
> 1 medium head green cabbage, shredded
> 1/2 cup uncooked rice
> 8 oz tomato sauce
> 1 cup water

1. Heat the oven to 350 degrees. In a medium skillet, brown the ground beef and onion. Drain the beef mixture and transfer it to a baking dish.

2. Spread the shredded cabbage evenly over the beef. Sprinkle the rice over the mixture and add the tomato sauce and water. Bake for 50 minutes or until the rice is tender.

Exchanges
1/2 Starch
2 Vegetable
1 Lean Meat
1 Fat

Calories 193
   Calories from Fat . . 72
Total Fat . . . . 8 g
   Saturated Fat . . . . . . 3 g
Cholesterol . . . . 36 mg
Sodium . . . . 225 mg
Carbohydrate . . . . . . 18 g
   Dietary Fiber . . . . . . 3 g
   Sugars . . . . 4 g
Protein . . . . 13 g

Collard Greens

Preparation time: 20 minutes
Serves 8   Serving size: 1 cup

>   4 lb collard greens
>   3 cups reduced-sodium, reduced-fat chicken both
>   2 medium onions, chopped
>   3 whole garlic cloves, crushed
>   1 tsp red pepper flakes
>   1 tsp pepper

1. Wash and cut the collard greens and place them in a large stockpot. Add the remaining ingredients and enough water to cover.

2. Cook until tender, stirring occasionally, about 3 1/2 hours. The flavors will blend even more if you let the greens sit for a bit after cooking.

Exchanges

3 Vegetable

Calories 78
   Calories from Fat . . . 4
Total Fat . . . . 0 g
   Saturated Fat . . . . . . 0 g
Cholesterol . . . . 0 mg
Sodium . . . . 240 mg
Carbohydrate . . . . . . 16 g
   Dietary Fiber . . . . . . 6 g
   Sugars . . . . 3 g
Protein . . . . 4 g

Collards with Smoked Turkey

Preparation time: 20 minutes
Serves 8   Serving size: 1 cup

> 4 lb collard greens
>
> 1/4 lb smoked turkey breast
>
> 3 cups reduced-sodium, reduced-fat chicken broth
>
> 2 medium onions, chopped
>
> 3 whole garlic cloves, crushed
>
> 1 tsp red pepper flakes
>
> 1 tsp pepper

1. Wash and cut the collard greens and place them in a large stockpot. Add the remaining ingredients and enough water to cover.

2. Cook until tender, stirring occasionally, about 3 1/2 hours. The flavors will blend even more if you let the greens sit for a bit after cooking.

Exchanges
3 Vegetable

Calories 91
   Calories from Fat . . . 6
Total Fat . . . . 1 g
   Saturated Fat . . . . . . 0 g
Cholesterol . . . . 7 mg
Sodium . . . . 410 mg
Carbohydrate . . . . . . 16 g
   Dietary Fiber . . . . . . 6 g
   Sugars . . . . 3 g
Protein . . . . 7 g

Creamed Potatoes

Preparation time: 15 minutes
Serves 6   Serving size: 1/2 cup

1 lb potatoes, washed, peeled, and cut into quarters

1 cup evaporated fat-free (skim) milk

2 tsp reduced-fat margarine

2 Tbsp chives

1 tsp salt

1 tsp white pepper

3 Tbsp water

1. Boil the potatoes for 20–30 minutes or until done.

2. Drain the potatoes and add the remaining ingredients. Whip well.

Exchanges
1 Starch

Calories 91
    Calories from Fat . . . 7
Total Fat . . . . 1 g
    Saturated Fat . . . . . . 0 g
Cholesterol . . . . 2 mg
Sodium . . . . 450 mg
Carbohydrate . . . . . . 17 g
    Dietary Fiber . . . . . . 1 g
    Sugars . . . . 5 g
Protein . . . . 4 g

Field Peas

Preparation time: 10 minutes
Serves 6   Serving size: 1 cup

- 2 cups water
- 8 oz fresh chicken or turkey necks
- 1 medium onion, chopped
- 1 clove garlic, minced
- 1 tsp parsley
- 1 lb fresh or frozen field peas
- 1/2 tsp salt
- 1/4 tsp red pepper flakes
- Pepper to taste (optional)

1. In a large stockpot, boil the water. Add the chicken or turkey necks, onion, garlic, and parsley and boil for 15 minutes.

2. Add the field peas and cook until tender, about 30 minutes. Add the salt, pepper flakes, and pepper. Serve over steamed rice.

Exchanges
1 1/2 Starch
1 Very Lean Meat

Calories 148
    Calories from Fat . . 16
Total Fat . . . . 2 g
    Saturated Fat . . . . . . 1 g
Cholesterol . . . . 23 mg
Sodium . . . . 207 mg
Carbohydrate . . . . . . 22 g
    Dietary Fiber . . . . . . 7 g
    Sugars . . . . 3 g
Protein . . . . 12 g

Fried Green Tomatoes

Preparation time: 10 minutes
Serves 4   Serving size: 4 slices

> 4 firm green tomatoes
> 1 cup cornmeal
>   Salt to taste (optional)
>   Pepper to taste (optional)
> 3 Tbsp canola oil

1. Wash the tomatoes, remove the stems, and slice each tomato into 4 thick slices. Season the cornmeal with salt and pepper.

2. Heat the oil in a medium skillet until hot. Dip the tomato slices into the cornmeal and fry until brown, turning once, about 3–4 minutes total.

Exchanges
2 Starch
2 Monounsaturated Fat

Calories	251
Calories from Fat	102
Total Fat	11 g
Saturated Fat	0 g
Cholesterol	0 mg
Sodium	17 mg
Carbohydrate	33 g
Dietary Fiber	4 g
Sugars	3 g
Protein	4 g

Fried Okra

Preparation time: 10 minutes
Serves 6   Serving size: 1/2 cup

      1 lb fresh okra
      1 cup egg substitute
    1/8 tsp salt
      2 Tbsp water
      1 cup yellow cornmeal
    1/4 cup canola oil
         Salt to taste (optional)
         Pepper to taste (optional)

1. Wash the okra, trim the ends, and cut each piece in half. Beat egg substitute, salt, and water. Dip the okra into the egg mixture and roll in the cornmeal to coat.

2. Heat the oil in a medium skillet until hot. Fry the okra until brown, about 10–15 minutes. Season with salt and pepper to taste.

Exchanges
1 1/2 Starch
1 Vegetable
2 Monounsaturated Fat

Calories	244
Calories from Fat	. 117
Total Fat	13 g
Saturated Fat	0 g
Cholesterol	0 mg
Sodium	126 mg
Carbohydrate	24 g
Dietary Fiber	3 g
Sugars	2 g
Protein	8 g

Garlic Mashed Potatoes

Preparation time: 10 minutes
Serves 6   Serving size: 1/2 cup

4 medium potatoes, peeled and cubed

7 cloves garlic, minced

1/3 cup fat-free (skim) milk, heated

1/4 cup fat-free sour cream

2 Tbsp reduced-fat margarine

Salt to taste (optional)

Pepper to taste (optional)

1. Boil the potatoes over medium heat until tender and drain them.

2. Add the garlic and mash the potatoes. Add the milk, sour cream, margarine, salt, and pepper and mix well until smooth.

Exchanges
1 Starch
1/2 Fat

Calories 99
   Calories from Fat . . 18
Total Fat . . . . 2 g
   Saturated Fat . . . . . . 0 g
Cholesterol . . . . 0 mg
Sodium . . . . 61 mg
Carbohydrate . . . . . . 18 g
   Dietary Fiber . . . . . . 1 g
   Sugars . . . . 4 g
Protein . . . . 3 g

Green Beans and New Potatoes

Preparation time: 10 minutes
Serves 6   Serving size: 1 cup

- 2 16-oz bags frozen green beans
- 8 new potatoes, washed, peeled, and halved
- 1 medium onion, chopped
- 4 oz smoked turkey breast

1. Add all ingredients to a large stockpot and cover with water. Bring to a boil, then reduce heat.

2. Cook until the green beans and new potatoes are tender, about 20 minutes.

Exchanges
1 Starch
2 Vegetable

Calories 117
   Calories from Fat . . . 5
Total Fat . . . . 1 g
   Saturated Fat . . . . . . 0 g
Cholesterol . . . . 9 mg
Sodium . . . . 242 mg
Carbohydrate . . . . . . 23 g
   Dietary Fiber . . . . . . 5 g
   Sugars . . . . 6 g
Protein . . . . 7 g

Luscious Lima Beans

Preparation time: 10 minutes
Serves 8   Serving size: 1/2 cup

4 oz smoked turkey breast
2 8-oz bags frozen lima beans
1 medium onion, chopped
1 clove garlic, minced

1. Put the turkey into a medium pot and cover with water. Boil for 30 minutes.

2. Add the remaining ingredients and cook until the lima beans are tender, about 20 minutes. Serve with corn bread (see recipe on page 118).

Exchanges
1 Starch

Calories 83
  Calories from Fat . . . 4
Total Fat . . . . 0 g
  Saturated Fat . . . . . . 0 g
Cholesterol . . . . 7 mg
Sodium . . . . 204 mg
Carbohydrate . . . . . . 14 g
  Dietary Fiber . . . . . . 4 g
  Sugars . . . . 3 g
Protein . . . . 7 g

Orange Carrots

Preparation time: 5 minutes
Serves 8   Serving size: 1/2 cup

2 lb baby carrots

2 Tbsp brown sugar

2 Tbsp reduced-fat margarine

1/4 cup orange juice concentrate, thawed

1/2 cup mandarin orange pieces

1/4 tsp salt

1 medium Vidalia onion, thinly sliced

1. Heat the oven to 350 degrees. Boil the carrots until tender and drain them.

2. In a separate bowl, combine the remaining ingredients and mix well. Place the carrots in a baking dish and cover with the sauce.

3. Stir once to coat the carrots. Bake for 15–20 minutes.

Exchanges
3 Vegetable
1/2 Fat

Calories 95
   Calories from Fat . . 14
Total Fat . . . . 2 g
   Saturated Fat . . . . . . 0 g
Cholesterol . . . . 0 mg
Sodium . . . . 166 mg
Carbohydrate . . . . . . 20 g
   Dietary Fiber . . . . . . 4 g
   Sugars . . . . 12 g
Protein . . . . 2 g

Orange Sweet Potatoes

Preparation time: 20 minutes
Serves 8   Serving size: 1/2 cup

> 5 medium oranges, unpeeled
> 1/3 cup brown sugar
> 1/2 cup brandy
> 1/4 cup evaporated fat-free (skim) milk
> 2 Tbsp reduced-fat margarine
> 1/2 tsp salt
> 4 cups cooked, mashed sweet potatoes
> Dash nutmeg

1. Grate the peel from one orange. Cut the remaining oranges in half. Scoop out the pulp to yield 2 cups of drained fruit and save the shells.

2. Cut a thin slice from the bottom of each orange shell to make it sit flat. Sprinkle the orange pulp with brown sugar and set aside.

3. Heat the oven to 350 degrees. In a medium saucepan, heat the brandy, evaporated milk, margarine, and salt. Add to the sweet potatoes and mix well.

4. Stuff each of the 8 orange shells with 1/2 cup of the sweet potato mixture. Sprinkle each shell with grated orange peel. Bake for 30 minutes. Garnish with a dash of nutmeg.

Exchanges
2 1/2 Carbohydrate

Calories 189
　Calories from Fat . . 14
Total Fat . . . . 2 g
　Saturated Fat . . . . . . 0 g
Cholesterol . . . . 0 mg
Sodium . . . . 191 mg
Carbohydrate . . . . . . 40 g
　Dietary Fiber . . . . . . 4 g
　Sugars . . . . 25 g
Protein . . . . 3 g

Rutabaga Soufflé

Preparation time: 15 minutes
Serves 8   Serving size: 1/2 cup

1   large rutabaga
1   tsp sugar
1   cup reduced-fat sour cream
2   Tbsp reduced-fat margarine
1   tsp baking powder
    Salt to taste (optional)
    Pepper to taste (optional)
2   eggs, separated, or 1/2 cup egg substitute
1/2   cup dried breadcrumbs
    Dash nutmeg

1. Peel the rutabaga and boil in a saucepan with the sugar and enough water to cover for 20–30 minutes. Drain and mash the rutabaga to yield 2 cups.

2. Heat the oven to 350 degrees. In a medium bowl, combine the rutabaga, sour cream, margarine, baking powder, salt, pepper, and egg yolks.

3. In a separate bowl, beat the egg whites until stiff. Fold the egg white into the rutabaga mixture. Pour into 1 1/2-quart casserole dish. Sprinkle with the breadcrumbs and nutmeg.

4. Bake for 30 minutes.

Exchanges
1/2 Starch
1 Vegetable
1 Fat

Calories 112
   Calories from Fat . . 49
Total Fat . . . . 5 g
   Saturated Fat . . . . . . 2 g
Cholesterol . . . . 63 mg
Sodium . . . . 166 mg
Carbohydrate . . . . . . 12 g
   Dietary Fiber . . . . . . 1 g
   Sugars . . . . 5 g
Protein . . . . 4 g

Smothered Cabbage

Preparation time: 20 minutes
Serves 6   Serving size: 1 cup

> 1 medium head green cabbage
>
> 1 Tbsp canola oil
>
> 1 medium green bell pepper, seeded and chopped
>
> 1 tsp caraway seeds
>
> 1/8 tsp salt
>
> Pepper to taste (optional)

1. Wash and quarter the cabbage and pat dry. Heat the oil in a large skillet. Add the bell pepper and saute until limp, about 5 minutes.

2. Add the cabbage, caraway seeds, salt, and pepper. Cover tightly and cook over medium heat until the cabbage is just tender (cabbage becomes mushy when overcooked), about 15–20 minutes.

Exchanges
1 Vegetable
1/2 Monounsaturated Fat

Calories	60
Calories from Fat	27
Total Fat	3 g
Saturated Fat	0 g
Cholesterol	0 mg
Sodium	58 mg
Carbohydrate	8 g
Dietary Fiber	4 g
Sugars	3 g
Protein	2 g

Steamed Cabbage

Preparation time: 10 minutes
Serves 6   Serving size: 1 cup

  1 Tbsp olive oil

  3 oz smoked turkey, cut into pieces

1/3 cup water

  1 medium head cabbage, chopped

1/8 tsp salt

1/8 tsp pepper

1. Heat the oil in a large saucepan and saute the turkey for 5 minutes.

2. Add the remaining ingredients and cook the cabbage just until tender (cabbage becomes mushy when overcooked), about 15–20 minutes.

Exchanges
1 Vegetable
1/2 Fat

Calories 65
   Calories from Fat . . 27
Total Fat . . . . 3 g
   Saturated Fat . . . . . . 1 g
Cholesterol . . . . 7 mg
Sodium . . . . 228 mg
Carbohydrate . . . . . . 6 g
   Dietary Fiber . . . . . . 3 g
   Sugars . . . . 2 g
Protein . . . . 4 g

Stewed Tomatoes and Okra

Preparation time: 15 minutes
Serves 8   Serving size: 1 cup

  8 large fresh tomatoes

  2 tsp reduced-fat margarine

  2 medium onions, chopped

  1 green bell pepper, seeded and chopped

 16 oz frozen or fresh okra

  1 cup frozen corn

  2 tsp sugar

1/2 cup dried breadcrumbs

1. Plunge tomatoes in boiling water for 1 minute to make them easier to peel. Peel and chop the tomatoes.

2. Heat the margarine in a large skillet and saute the tomatoes, onions, and bell pepper. Add the okra, corn, and sugar and simmer for 25 minutes. To thicken, add the breadcrumbs and stir well.

Exchanges
1 Starch
2 Vegetable

Calories 128
   Calories from Fat . . 20
Total Fat . . . . 2 g
   Saturated Fat . . . . . . 0 g
Cholesterol . . . . 0 mg
Sodium . . . . 85 mg
Carbohydrate . . . . . . 26 g
   Dietary Fiber . . . . . . 5 g
   Sugars . . . . 10 g
Protein . . . . 5 g

Sweet Potato Soufflé

Preparation time: 25 minutes
Serves 6   Serving size: 1/2 cup

4	lb sweet potatoes
2	Tbsp sugar
1/2	cup brown sugar
1/4	cup raisins
1	tsp nutmeg
1/2	cup evaporated fat-free (skim) milk
1/3	cup reduced-fat margarine
1	cup egg substitute
1/4	cup chopped pecans
1/2	tsp salt
	Juice of 1 lemon
1/2	cup miniature marshmallows

1. Peel and boil the sweet potatoes. Heat the oven to 350 degrees.

2. Drain and mash the sweet potatoes. Place them in a large bowl and add all ingredients. Stir well.

3. Spray a casserole dish with nonstick cooking spray. Place the sweet potatoes in the casserole dish and bake for 30 minutes.

4. Change the oven setting to broil, sprinkle the marshmallows over the sweet potatoes, and place under broiler until the marshmallows melt.

Exchanges
3 Carbohydrate
1/2 Fat

Calories 238
  Calories from Fat . . 38
Total Fat . . . . 4 g
  Saturated Fat . . . . . . 0 g
Cholesterol . . . . 0 mg
Sodium . . . . 203 mg
Carbohydrate . . . . . . 46 g
  Dietary Fiber . . . . . . 4 g
  Sugars . . . . 29 g
Protein . . . . 5 g

Turnip Greens with Bottoms

Preparation time: 20 minutes
Serves 8   Serving size: 1 cup

  2 large bunches turnip greens with turnips
  8 oz smoked turkey breast
  1 large onion, chopped
     Red pepper flakes

1. Wash the turnip greens thoroughly and cut into pieces. Peel the turnips and chop into small pieces.

2. Boil the turkey in water until the turkey is tender, about 20 minutes. Add the turnip greens, turnips, onion, and red pepper flakes and cook until done, about 20 minutes.

Exchanges
1 Vegetable
1 Very Lean Meat

Calories 59
  Calories from Fat . . . 5
Total Fat . . . . 1 g
  Saturated Fat . . . . . . 0 g
Cholesterol . . . . 13 mg
Sodium . . . . 394 mg
Carbohydrate . . . . . . 8 g
  Dietary Fiber . . . . . . 4 g
  Sugars . . . . 4 g
Protein . . . . 7 g

---

*B*reads, Cereals, and Grains

Baked Cheese Grits

Preparation time: 20 minutes
Serves 6   Serving size: 1 cup

4 cups water

1/2 tsp salt

1 cup grits

3 Tbsp flour

1 cup shredded reduced-fat cheddar cheese

1/4 cup chopped green onion

1 tsp minced garlic

1 cup egg substitute

1. Boil the water and add the salt and grits. Cook, covered, over low heat for 20 minutes. Meanwhile, heat the oven to 350 degrees.

2. Stir the flour, cheese, green onion, garlic, and egg substitute into the grits. Pour into a nonstick baking pan and bake for 30 minutes.

Exchanges
1 1/2 Starch
1 Lean Meat

Calories 187
   Calories from Fat . . 39
Total Fat . . . . 4 g
   Saturated Fat . . . . . . 3 g
Cholesterol . . . . 13 mg
Sodium . . . . 422 mg
Carbohydrate . . . . . . 24 g
   Dietary Fiber . . . . . . 2 g
   Sugars . . . . 1 g
Protein . . . . 13 g

Banana Bread

Preparation time: 20 minutes
Serves 10   Serving size: 1 slice

1 1/2	cups flour
1 1/2	tsp baking powder
1/4	tsp baking soda
1/4	tsp cinnamon
1/4	tsp nutmeg
1/8	tsp salt
1	egg
3	medium soft bananas, mashed
3/4	cup sugar
1/4	cup canola oil
1	tsp finely shredded lemon peel
1/4	cup coconut flakes

1. Spray a 2 × 4 × 2-inch loaf pan with nonstick cooking spray and heat the oven to 350 degrees. In a medium mixing bowl, combine the flour, baking powder, baking soda, cinnamon, nutmeg, and salt. Make a well in the center of the dry mixture and set aside.

2. In a blender or food processor, combine the egg, bananas, sugar, oil, lemon peel, and coconut. Add the egg mixture all at once to the dry mixture. Stir just until moistened (do not overbeat).

3. Spoon the batter into the prepared pan. Bake for 50–55 minutes or until a wooden toothpick inserted near the center comes out clean. Remove from the pan and cool on a wire rack.

Exchanges
2 1/2 Carbohydrate
1 Monounsaturated Fat

Calories 227
  Calories from Fat . . 63
Total Fat . . . . 7 g
  Saturated Fat . . . . . . 1 g
Cholesterol . . . . 21 mg
Sodium . . . . 126 mg
Carbohydrate . . . . . . 39 g
  Dietary Fiber . . . . . . 1 g
  Sugars . . . . 22 g
Protein . . . . 3 g

Charlie's Corn Casserole

Preparation time: 15 minutes
Serves 8   Serving size: 1/2 cup

- 1 8-oz can creamed corn
- 1 cup canned whole kernel corn, undrained
- 2 tsp sugar
- 1 cup egg substitute
- 1 6 1/2-oz pkg corn bread mix
- 1 Tbsp corn oil

1. Heat the oven to 350 degrees. In a large bowl, mix all the ingredients together, including the liquid from the corn.

2. Pour the batter into a nonstick loaf pan and bake for 45 minutes or until puffed and golden.

Exchanges
2 Starch

Calories	156
Calories from Fat	25
Total Fat	3 g
Saturated Fat	1 g
Cholesterol	0 mg
Sodium	337 mg
Carbohydrate	29 g
Dietary Fiber	2 g
Sugars	9 g
Protein	6 g

Corn Bread

Preparation time: 15 minutes
Serves 8   Serving size: 1 piece

1	cup yellow cornmeal
1/2	cup flour
2	tsp baking powder
1/2	tsp salt
1 1/2	cups fat-free (skim) milk
1	cup egg substitute
1	Tbsp canola oil

1. Heat the oven to 425 degrees. In a large bowl, mix the dry ingredients together. Add the milk, egg substitute, and oil to the dry ingredients and mix well.

2. Pour the batter into a 13 × 9-inch nonstick loaf pan and bake for 30 minutes.

Exchanges
1 1/2 Starch

Calories 142
   Calories from Fat . . 20
Total Fat . . . . 2 g
   Saturated Fat . . . . . . 0 g
Cholesterol . . . . 1 mg
Sodium . . . . 315 mg
Carbohydrate . . . . . . 23 g
   Dietary Fiber . . . . . . 1 g
   Sugars . . . . 3 g
Protein . . . . 7 g

Corn Bread Casserole

Preparation time: 15 minutes
Serves 6   Serving size: 1/2 cup

  1 cup yellow cornmeal
1/2 tsp baking soda
1/4 tsp salt
  8 oz plain fat-free yogurt
  1 8-oz can creamed corn
1/4 cup evaporated fat-free (skim) milk

1. Heat the oven to 350 degrees. In a large bowl, combine the dry ingredients. Add the remaining ingredients and stir just until moistened (do not overbeat).

2. Pour the batter into 6 individual soufflé cups and bake for 30 minutes or until a knife inserted in the cups comes out clean. Serve hot.

Exchanges
2 Starch

Calories 138
  Calories from Fat . . . 5
Total Fat . . . . 1 g
  Saturated Fat . . . . . . 0 g
Cholesterol . . . . 1 mg
Sodium . . . . 351 mg
Carbohydrate . . . . . . 29 g
  Dietary Fiber . . . . . . 2 g
  Sugars . . . . 7 g
Protein . . . . 5 g

Corn Bread Dressing

Preparation time: 25 minutes
Serves 10   Serving size: 1/2 cup

> 3 Tbsp reduced-fat margarine
> 1 cup chopped onion
> 2 cups chopped celery
> 2 cloves garlic, crushed
> 1/4 cup parsley
> 6 slices whole-wheat bread, dried
> 5 cups leftover cornbread (see recipe, page 118)
> 1 tsp thyme
> 2 tsp sage
> 1 tsp marjoram
> 1 tsp pepper
> 1/2 tsp salt
> 2 cups egg substitute
> 2 cups turkey broth (from boiling giblets without salt, or use canned)

1. Heat the margarine in a large skillet and saute the onion, celery, garlic, and parsley for 10 minutes. Put the whole-wheat bread and corn bread in a large bowl and crumble up into small pieces.

2. Heat the oven to 350 degrees. Add the spices to the bread and mix well. Add the onion mixture and stir.

3. Add the egg substitute and mix well, then add cool turkey broth and stir. Pour the dressing into a nonstick baking pan and bake for 45 minutes. For variety, try adding chestnuts, mushrooms, olives, or reduced-fat sausage to this dressing.

Exchanges
2 Starch
1 Monounsaturated Fat

Calories 212
   Calories from Fat . . 38
Total Fat . . . . 4 g
   Saturated Fat . . . . . . 0 g
Cholesterol . . . . 1 mg
Sodium . . . . 585 mg
Carbohydrate . . . . . . 30 g
   Dietary Fiber . . . . . . 3 g
   Sugars . . . . 5 g
Protein . . . . 13 g

Corn Muffins

Preparation time: 15 minutes
Serves 12   Serving size: 1 muffin

> 1 cup yellow cornmeal
> 1 cup boiling water
> 1/2 tsp salt
> 2 tsp baking powder
> 2 tsp reduced-fat margarine
> 1/2 cup fat-free (skim) milk
> 1/2 cup egg substitute
> 2 tsp sugar

1. In a large bowl, pour the boiling water over the cornmeal and stir well. Allow to cool.

2. Heat the oven to 425 degrees. Add all ingredients to the bowl, mix, pour the batter into nonstick muffin pans, and bake for 25 minutes or until light brown.

Exchanges
1/2 Starch

Calories	57
Calories from Fat	5
Total Fat	1 g
Saturated Fat	0 g
Cholesterol	0 mg
Sodium	186 mg
Carbohydrate	11 g
Dietary Fiber	1 g
Sugars	1 g
Protein	2 g

Corn Pudding

Preparation time: 20 minutes
Serves 8   Serving size: 1/2 cup

      2 cups grated fresh corn kernels (about 12 ears)
      1 Tbsp flour
      1 Tbsp sugar
      1 tsp salt
    1/4 tsp pepper
      1 cup egg substitute
      1 cup evaporated fat-free (skim) milk
      1 Tbsp reduced-fat margarine

1. Grate the corn from the ears into a large bowl. Add the flour, sugar, salt, and pepper to the corn and stir.

2. Heat the oven to 325 degrees. In a separate bowl, beat the egg substitute and milk for 3 minutes and add to the corn mixture.

3. Pour the pudding into a nonstick loaf pan and place in the oven in a hot water bath. Bake for 30 minutes or until the pudding is firm to the touch.

Exchanges
1 Starch

Calories 103
  Calories from Fat . . 12
Total Fat . . . . 1 g
  Saturated Fat . . . . . . 0 g
Cholesterol . . . . 1 mg
Sodium . . . . 401 mg
Carbohydrate . . . . . . 17 g
  Dietary Fiber . . . . . . 1 g
  Sugars . . . . 6 g
Protein . . . . 7 g

Dill Drop Biscuits

Preparation time: 15 minutes
Serves 8   Serving size: 1 biscuit

> 1 cup unbleached flour
> 2 tsp baking powder
> 1/4 tsp salt
> 1 tsp dill
> 1/2 cup low-fat buttermilk
> 1/4 cup canola oil

1. Heat the oven to 425 degrees. Place the dry ingredients in a medium bowl. Add the buttermilk and oil and stir just enough to moisten the dry ingredients.

2. Drop tablespoonfuls of batter onto a nonstick baking sheet and bake for 15 minutes. Serve hot.

Exchanges
1 Starch
1 Monounsaturated Fat

Calories 128
Calories from Fat . . 66
Total Fat . . . . 7 g
Saturated Fat . . . . . . 0 g
Cholesterol . . . . 1 mg
Sodium . . . . 180 mg
Carbohydrate . . . . . . 13 g
Dietary Fiber . . . . . . 0 g
Sugars . . . . 1 g
Protein . . . . 2 g

Doc's French Toast

Preparation time: 10 minutes
Serves 8   Serving size: 1 slice

> 2 cups egg substitute
>
> 2 Tbsp sugar
>
> 1/2 tsp cinnamon
>
> 1/2 tsp nutmeg
>
> 1 tsp vanilla extract
>
> 8 slices white bread

1. Mix the batter ingredients together in a medium bowl and stir well. Dip the bread slices into the batter and turn quickly to coat both sides evenly.

2. Place on a hot nonstick griddle and brown. Serve with reduced-calorie syrup or fresh fruit.

Exchanges
1 Starch
1 Very Lean Meat

Calories 101
   Calories from Fat . . . 8
Total Fat . . . . 1 g
   Saturated Fat . . . . . . 0 g
Cholesterol . . . . 0 mg
Sodium . . . . 218 mg
Carbohydrate . . . . . . 15 g
   Dietary Fiber . . . . . . 1 g
   Sugars . . . . 5 g
Protein . . . . 8 g

Ernestine's Pigeon Peas and Rice

Preparation time: 20 minutes
Serves 8   Serving size: 1/2 cup

- 1 Tbsp canola oil
- 1 medium onion, chopped
- 1 medium green bell pepper, seeded and chopped
- 1 can pigeon peas (check the Hispanic food aisle in your supermarket)
- 8 oz tomato sauce
- 1 cup water
- 1/2 tsp thyme
- 2 bay leaves
- 3/4 tsp salt
- 1/2 tsp pepper
- 1 tsp garlic powder
- 2 cups cooked rice

1. Heat the oil in a large saucepan and saute the onion and bell pepper until slightly tender. Add the peas, tomato sauce, water, thyme, bay leaves, salt, pepper, and garlic powder and simmer 3 minutes.

2. Add the rice and stir well. Heat for 2 minutes or until the rice is hot.

Exchanges
1 1/2 Starch
1 Vegetable

Calories	135
Calories from Fat	19
Total Fat	2 g
Saturated Fat	0 g
Cholesterol	0 mg
Sodium	492 mg
Carbohydrate	25 g
Dietary Fiber	4 g
Sugars	4 g
Protein	4 g

Hoe Cake

Preparation time: 10 minutes
Serves 6   Serving size: 1 pancake

1   cup cornmeal
1   cup flour
2   tsp baking powder
1/2   tsp salt
2   Tbsp canola oil
Cold water

1. Combine all dry ingredients and oil in a large bowl and add enough cold water to make a soft batter.

2. Spray a nonstick griddle with nonstick cooking spray and heat to medium heat. Pour the batter into the griddle and cook until done, turning once to brown both sides. Slice to serve.

Exchanges
2 Starch
1 Monounsaturated Fat

Calories 204
　Calories from Fat . . 47
Total Fat . . . . 5 g
　Saturated Fat . . . . . . 0 g
Cholesterol . . . . 0 mg
Sodium . . . . 316 mg
Carbohydrate . . . . . . 35 g
　Dietary Fiber . . . . . . 2 g
　Sugars . . . . 0 g
Protein . . . . 4 g

Hoppin' John

Preparation time: 15 minutes
Serves 6   Serving size: 1 cup

1 lb dried black-eyed peas

2 qt water

1 medium onion, chopped

1 lb smoked turkey breast, chopped

Red pepper flakes to taste (optional)

1 cup cooked rice

1. Soak the black-eyed peas overnight in cold water, or boil for 2 minutes and then soak for 1 hour. Drain.

2. Place the peas in a large stockpot and add the water, onion, smoked turkey, and red pepper flakes. Simmer for 2 hours or until the peas are soft.

3. Stir in the rice or serve it on the side. (To reduce the sodium content of this recipe, use ground turkey breast instead of smoked turkey.)

Exchanges
3 1/2 Starch
3 Very Lean Meat

Calories 365
    Calories from Fat . . 17
Total Fat . . . . 2 g
    Saturated Fat . . . . . . 0 g
Cholesterol . . . . 35 mg
Sodium . . . . 920 mg
Carbohydrate . . . . . . 55 g
    Dietary Fiber . . . . . . 8 g
    Sugars . . . . 7 g
Protein . . . . 34 g

John's Garlic Rice

Preparation time: 15 minutes
Serves 8   Serving size: 1/2 cup

2 Tbsp reduced-fat margarine

2 Tbsp minced garlic

2 cups long-grain rice

4 cups reduced-sodium, reduced-fat chicken broth

Salt to taste (optional)

Pepper to taste (optional)

1. Heat the margarine in a large skillet and saute the garlic and rice, stirring constantly, until lightly brown.

2. Add the chicken broth, salt, and pepper and stir. Bring to a boil, then reduce heat to simmer, cover, and cook for 20 minutes.

Exchanges
2 1/2 Starch

Calories	192
Calories from Fat	. . 15
Total Fat	2 g
Saturated Fat	0 g
Cholesterol	0 mg
Sodium	301 mg
Carbohydrate	38 g
Dietary Fiber	1 g
Sugars	1 g
Protein	4 g

Barbecue Pulled Pork, *p. 33*
Soul Slaw, *p. 156*

Apple and Blueberry Tart, *p. 177*

Corn Soup, Cajun Style, *p. 139*
Corn Muffins, *p. 121*

Orange Sweet Potatoes, *p. 106*

Red Rice

Preparation time: 15 minutes
Serves 6   Serving size: 1/2 cup

- 2 cups water
- 1 chicken-flavored bouillon cube
- 1 medium onion, chopped
- 1 cup uncooked rice
- 2 cloves garlic, minced
- 1/2 8-oz can tomato sauce
- 1 green bell pepper, seeded and chopped

1. Boil the water in a large saucepan. Add the bouillon cube and stir.

2. Add the remaining ingredients, stir well, and return to a boil. Reduce the heat to simmer and cook, covered, for 20 minutes.

Exchanges
2 Starch

Calories	137
Calories from Fat	3
Total Fat	0 g
Saturated Fat	0 g
Cholesterol	0 mg
Sodium	222 mg
Carbohydrate	30 g
Dietary Fiber	1 g
Sugars	4 g
Protein	3 g

Spanish Rice

Preparation time: 15 minutes
Serves 8   Serving size: 1/2 cup

2 Tbsp reduced-fat margarine

1 cup uncooked rice

1 medium onion, finely chopped

1/4 cup chopped celery

1 clove garlic, crushed

1 green bell pepper, seeded and chopped

2 cups water

1 14-oz can crushed tomatoes, undrained

1 tsp salt

1/4 tsp pepper

1. Heat the margarine in a large saucepan and saute the rice, onion, celery, garlic, and bell pepper until the rice is lightly brown.

2. Add the water, tomatoes, salt, and pepper and bring to a boil. Reduce the heat to simmer and cook, covered, for 20 minutes.

Exchanges
1 1/2 Starch

Calories 130
  Calories from Fat . . 15
Total Fat . . . . 2 g
  Saturated Fat . . . . . . 0 g
Cholesterol . . . . 0 mg
Sodium . . . . 455 mg
Carbohydrate . . . . . . 26 g
  Dietary Fiber . . . . . . 2 g
  Sugars . . . . 4 g
Protein . . . . 3 g

Spoon Bread

Preparation time: 15 minutes
Serves 6   Serving size: 1 slice

- 1 cup boiling water
- 1 cup yellow cornmeal
- 1/2 tsp salt
- 2 tsp reduced-fat margarine
- 1 tsp baking powder
- 2 eggs, separated
- 1 1/2 cups fat-free (skim) milk

1. In a large heatproof bowl, pour the boiling water over the cornmeal and stir well. Stir the salt and margarine into the cornmeal and allow to cool.

2. Heat the oven to 375 degrees. Add the baking powder, egg yolks, and milk to the bowl and stir. Beat the egg whites until stiff peaks are formed and fold into the batter.

3. Pour the batter into a nonstick loaf pan and bake for 45 minutes.

Exchanges
1 1/2 Starch

Calories 137
    Calories from Fat . . 25
Total Fat . . . . 3 g
    Saturated Fat . . . . . . 1 g
Cholesterol . . . . 72 mg
Sodium . . . . 318 mg
Carbohydrate . . . . . . 21 g
    Dietary Fiber . . . . . . 2 g
    Sugars . . . . 3 g
Protein . . . . 6 g

Sweet Potato Bread

Preparation time: 20 minutes
Serves 6   Serving size: 1 slice

2	large sweet potatoes, peeled
2	Tbsp reduced-fat margarine
3	Tbsp sugar
1	tsp nutmeg
1 1/2	tsp allspice
1/4	tsp salt
5	Tbsp flour
1	cup egg substitute

1. Boil the sweet potatoes until soft and mash thoroughly. Stir in the margarine.

2. Heat the oven to 425 degrees. Add all ingredients and mix thoroughly.

3. Pour the batter into a nonstick loaf pan and bake for 30 minutes, or until a knife inserted in the center comes out clean.

Exchanges
2 1/2 Starch

Calories 209
 Calories from Fat . . 18
Total Fat . . . . 2 g
 Saturated Fat . . . . . . 0 g
Cholesterol . . . . 0 mg
Sodium . . . . 212 mg
Carbohydrate . . . . . . 41 g
 Dietary Fiber . . . . . . 4 g
 Sugars . . . . 20 g
Protein . . . . 7 g

Soups and Salads

Black Bean Soup

Preparation time: 20 minutes
Serves 8   Serving size: 1 cup

1 lb dried black beans or 2 16-oz cans black beans, rinsed and drained

1 Tbsp canola oil

1 medium onion, chopped

4 cloves garlic, minced

1 carrot, shredded

1 green bell pepper, seeded and chopped

8 cups water

4 oz smoked turkey breast, diced

2 tsp oregano

1/2 tsp cumin

1/2 tsp pepper

1 tsp salt

2 Tbsp lemon juice

1. If using dried beans, soak them in water overnight. The next day, drain the beans.

2. In a large soup pot, heat the oil over medium heat. Add half the onion and all the garlic, carrot, and green pepper. Saute until the vegetables are soft. Stir in the beans and water. Add the turkey, oregano, cumin, and pepper.

3. Cover and simmer for 30 minutes, or until the beans are tender, stirring occasionally. Add the salt and lemon juice. Top with chopped onion to serve.

Exchanges

3 Starch
1 Very Lean Meat

Calories 225
 Calories from Fat . . 26
Total Fat . . . . 3 g
 Saturated Fat . . . . . . 0 g
Cholesterol . . . . 7 mg
Sodium . . . . 473 mg
Carbohydrate . . . . . . 42 g
 Dietary Fiber . . . . . 10 g
 Sugars . . . . 5 g
Protein . . . . 17 g

Cabbage and Chicken Soup

Preparation time: 20 minutes
Serves 8   Serving size: 1 cup

- 4 cups water
- 3 cups reduced-sodium, reduced-fat chicken broth
- 2 cups chopped fresh tomatoes
- 1/2 stalk celery, chopped
- 4 stalks green onion, chopped
- 1 medium potato, peeled and diced
- 1 bay leaf
- 1 tsp salt
- 1/2 tsp thyme
- 1/4 tsp caraway seeds
- 3 cups shredded cabbage
- 1 cup cooked chopped chicken
- 1 Tbsp lemon juice
- 2 tsp sugar

1. In a large soup pot, combine the water, broth, tomatoes, celery, onion, potato, bay leaf, salt, thyme, and caraway seeds.

2. Simmer for 30 minutes to 1 hour. Add the cabbage, chicken, lemon juice, and sugar. Remove the bay leaf and serve.

Exchanges

2 Vegetable
1 Very Lean Meat

Calories 81
  Calories from Fat . . 15
Total Fat . . . . 2 g
  Saturated Fat . . . . . . 1 g
Cholesterol . . . . 16 mg
Sodium . . . . 526 mg
Carbohydrate . . . . 9 g
  Dietary Fiber . . . . . . 2 g
  Sugars . . . . 4 g
Protein . . . . 7 g

Chicken Gumbo Soup

Preparation time: 30 minutes
Serves 6   Serving size: 1 cup

1	lb boneless, skinless chicken breast, diced
3	cups reduced-sodium, reduced-fat chicken broth, divided
3	cups water
1	cup chopped onion
1	clove garlic, minced
1	tsp salt
1/2	tsp pepper
1	bay leaf
1/8	tsp sage
1/4	tsp red pepper flakes
1/4	tsp thyme
1	cup chopped fresh tomatoes
1	cup corn kernels, frozen or fresh
1	cup frozen okra
2	Tbsp canola oil
1/4	cup flour
2	cups cooked brown rice

1. Place the chicken in a large soup pot with 1 cup of broth. Bring to a boil.

2. Add the additional broth, water, onion, garlic, salt (omit this if you need to reduce total sodium), pepper, bay leaf, sage, red pepper flakes, and thyme and simmer for 20 minutes.

3. Add the tomatoes, corn, and okra and simmer for 15 minutes.

4. In a separate pan, heat the oil and flour and stir until the flour and oil are golden brown and bubbly, stirring constantly. Add 1 cup of the soup broth to the mixture and whisk until smooth.

5. Add the mixture back to the soup pot and whisk until dissolved. Simmer 30 minutes. Stir in the rice the last 10 minutes of cooking.

Exchanges

2 Starch	2 Lean Meat

Calories 279
   Calories from Fat . . 61
Total Fat . . . . 7 g
   Saturated Fat . . . . . . 0 g
Cholesterol . . . . 43 mg
Sodium . . . . 720 mg
Carbohydrate . . . . . . 31 g
   Dietary Fiber . . . . . . 4 g
   Sugars . . . . 5 g
Protein . . . . 23 g

Chicken Noodle Soup

Preparation time: 20 minutes
Serves 8   Serving size: 1 cup

8	cups reduced-sodium, reduced-fat chicken broth
1 1/2	cups cooked diced chicken
3	carrots, sliced
2	medium onions, diced
2	Tbsp lite soy sauce
1	Tbsp dry sherry
1/2	tsp ginger
1	Tbsp parsley
4	oz uncooked whole-wheat noodles
4	stalks green onion, chopped

1. Place the chicken broth in a large pot and bring to a boil.

2. Add the chicken, carrots, onion, soy sauce (omit this if you need to reduce total sodium), sherry, ginger, and parsley. Reduce the heat and simmer for 10 minutes.

3. Add the noodles and simmer for 10 minutes more. Top with green onion to serve.

Exchanges
1 Starch
2 Very Lean Meat

Calories 157
    Calories from Fat . . 24
Total Fat . . . . 3 g
    Saturated Fat . . . . . . 1 g
Cholesterol . . . . 37 mg
Sodium . . . . 751 mg
Carbohydrate . . . . . . 18 g
    Dietary Fiber . . . . . . 2 g
    Sugars . . . . 5 g
Protein . . . . 13 g

Corn Soup, Cajun-Style

Preparation time: 30 minutes
Serves 12   Serving size: 1 cup

1	Tbsp canola oil
1 1/2	cups chopped onion
5	stalks green onion, sliced
1	cup chopped green bell pepper
2	cloves garlic, chopped
1/2	cup flour
5	cups water
4	chicken thighs, skinned, deboned, and chopped
1	14-oz can no-added-salt tomatoes, chopped (reserve juice)
2	cups chopped fresh tomatoes
6	oz tomato paste
1/8	tsp salt
1/8	tsp pepper
12	oz reduced-fat turkey sausage
32	oz frozen whole kernel corn
4	oz lean boneless ham

1. Heat the oil in a large soup pot and saute the onion, green onion, bell pepper, and garlic until tender. Add the flour and cook, stirring constantly, until bubbly.

2. Add the water, chicken, tomatoes and juice, tomato paste, salt, and pepper.

3. Brown the sausage in a separate skillet and drain. Add the sausage to the soup pot, along with the corn and ham. Bring to a boil, stirring frequently.

4. Reduce the heat and simmer, uncovered, for 1 hour, stirring occasionally.

Exchanges
1 1/2 Starch
2 Vegetable
1 Medium-Fat Meat

Calories 237
   Calories from Fat . . 62
Total Fat . . . . 7 g
   Saturated Fat . . . . . . 2 g
Cholesterol . . . . 38 mg
Sodium . . . . 487 mg
Carbohydrate . . . . . . 32 g
   Dietary Fiber . . . . . . 4 g
   Sugars . . . . 7 g
Protein . . . . 16 g

Cream of Broccoli Soup

Preparation time: 15 minutes
Serves 6   Serving size: 1 cup

> 1 1/2 cups water
> 3 cups finely chopped fresh broccoli
> 2 tsp canola oil
> 1 cup chopped onion
> 1 Tbsp chopped garlic
> 1 Tbsp flour
> 3 cups fat-free (skim) milk
> 1/2 tsp celery seeds
> 1 tsp salt
> 1/2 tsp pepper
> 1/8 tsp cayenne pepper
> 3/4 cup Parmesan cheese

1. Combine the water and the broccoli and boil over medium heat for 10 minutes. Remove from the heat and set aside.

2. In a large skillet, heat the oil and saute the onion and garlic until translucent, about 5 minutes.

3. Add the flour to the skillet, stirring constantly to mix. Add the liquid from the broccoli and cook until thickened, about 10 minutes.

4. Add the milk, broccoli, and spices and stir well (omit the salt if you need to reduce total sodium). Cook until hot, but do not allow the milk to boil. Top each serving with 1 Tbsp Parmesan cheese.

Exchanges

1 Skim Milk	1 Fat
1 Vegetable	

Calories 146
  Calories from Fat . . 46
Total Fat . . . . 5 g
  Saturated Fat . . . . . . 2 g
Cholesterol . . . . 10 mg
Sodium . . . . 658 mg
Carbohydrate . . . . . . 15 g
  Dietary Fiber . . . . . . 3 g
  Sugars . . . . 9 g
Protein . . . . 11 g

Seafood Chowder

Preparation time: 35 minutes
Serves 6   Serving size: 1 cup

    1 Tbsp reduced-fat margarine
1 1/2 cups chopped onion
    1 Tbsp chopped garlic
    2 Tbsp flour
    2 cups clam juice
    2 cups water
  1/2 cup chopped fresh parsley
2 1/2 cups chopped potatoes
    1 Tbsp thyme
  1/2 tsp salt
  1/2 tsp pepper
1 1/2 lb boneless, chopped flounder
    2 cups low-fat (1%) milk

1. In a large soup pot, melt the margarine and saute the onion and garlic until translucent, about 5 minutes. Stir in the flour and cook for 2 minutes, stirring constantly. Add the clam juice and water.

2. Bring to a boil, stirring constantly. Add all ingredients except the fish and the milk. Simmer until the vegetables are tender, about 10 minutes.

3. Add the fish and the milk and simmer just until the fish turns opaque. Be careful not to boil the milk. Serve hot.

Exchanges
1 1/2 Starch
3 Very Lean Meat

Calories 231
    Calories from Fat . . 34
Total Fat . . . . 4 g
    Saturated Fat . . . . . . 0 g
Cholesterol . . . . 40 mg
Sodium . . . . 469 mg
Carbohydrate . . . . . . 21 g
    Dietary Fiber . . . . . . 2 g
    Sugars . . . . 6 g
Protein . . . . 28 g

Soulful Chili

Preparation time: 20 minutes
Serves 8   Serving size: 1 cup

2 tsp canola oil

2 medium onions, chopped

2 cloves garlic, minced

1 green bell pepper, seeded and chopped

2 lb lean ground beef

2 1/2 cups cooked kidney beans, or 1 16-oz can kidney beans, rinsed and drained

6 oz tomato paste

1 tsp reduced-sodium beef bouillon powder or one cube

1 Tbsp Worcestershire sauce

1 tsp dry mustard

Red pepper flakes, to taste

3 Tbsp chili powder

Salt to taste (optional)

Pepper to taste (optional)

2 cups water

1. Heat the oil in a large soup pot and saute the onion, garlic, and bell pepper for 5 minutes. Stir in the beef and cook until done.

2. Add the remaining ingredients, cover, and simmer for 20 minutes.

Exchanges
1 1/2 Starch
3 Medium-Fat Meat

Calories 352
  Calories from Fat . 153
Total Fat . . . . 17 g
  Saturated Fat . . . . . . 6 g
Cholesterol . . . . 71 mg
Sodium . . . . 202 mg
Carbohydrate . . . . . . 24 g
  Dietary Fiber . . . . . . 6 g
  Sugars . . . . 5 g
Protein . . . . 23 g

Vegetable Soup with Noodles

Preparation time: 20 minutes
Serves 10   Serving size: 1 cup

1	Tbsp olive oil
2	cups chopped onion
1	green bell pepper, seeded and chopped
10	cups reduced-sodium, reduced-fat chicken broth
1	lb fresh carrots, sliced
1	cup chopped potatoes
1	cup fresh green beans, chopped
1	cup chopped fresh tomatoes
8	oz uncooked wide egg noodles
1/2	tsp pepper

1. Heat the oil in a large soup pot and saute the onion and bell pepper until tender.

2. Add the vegetables and simmer for 20 minutes.

3. Add the noodles and pepper and simmer for 10 minutes or until the pasta is cooked.

Exchanges
1 1/2 Starch
1 Vegetable

Calories 174
  Calories from Fat . . 23
Total Fat . . . . 3 g
  Saturated Fat . . . . . . 1 g
Cholesterol . . . . 22 mg
Sodium . . . . 588 mg
Carbohydrate . . . . . . 30 g
  Dietary Fiber . . . . . . 4 g
  Sugars . . . . 6 g
Protein . . . . 7 g

Vegetarian Bean Stew

Preparation time: 20 minutes
Serves 6   Serving size: 1 cup

1 Tbsp canola oil
1 medium onion, chopped
2 cloves garlic, minced
2 cups sliced zucchini
1 cup chopped green bell pepper
1 tsp oregano
1/4 tsp salt
1/8 tsp pepper
2 cups chopped fresh tomatoes
1 16-oz can kidney beans, rinsed and drained
2 cups cooked brown rice
1/2 cup reduced-fat cheddar cheese

1. Heat the oil in a large soup pot and saute the onion and garlic until tender. Add the zuchinni, green pepper, oregano, salt, and pepper. Cook for 5 minutes.

2. Add the tomatoes and beans, cover, and heat thoroughly, about 15 minutes. Spoon the mixture over hot rice and sprinkle with cheese to serve.

Exchanges

1 1/2 Starch	1 Fat
2 Vegetable	

Calories 219
　Calories from Fat . . 49
Total Fat . . . . 5 g
　Saturated Fat . . . . . . 1 g
Cholesterol . . . . 7 mg
Sodium . . . . 259 mg
Carbohydrate . . . . . . 34 g
　Dietary Fiber . . . . . . 6 g
　Sugars . . . . 7 g
Protein . . . . 10 g

Apple Slaw

Preparation time: 25 minutes
Serves 8   Serving size: 1/2 cup

   1/4 cup reduced-fat sour cream

     2 Tbsp sugar

   1/2 tsp salt

   1/2 tsp pepper

     1 tsp ground mustard

     2 lb unpeeled apples, julienned

     2 Tbsp lemon juice

     1 large head cabbage, julienned

1. In a large bowl, combine the sour cream, sugar, salt, pepper, and ground mustard. Mix well, cover, and chill for 1 hour.

2. Toss the apples with the lemon juice. Combine the apples and cabbage and mix well. Just before serving, add the dressing and toss.

Exchanges
1 1/2 Fruit
1 Vegetable

Calories 114
   Calories from Fat . . 12
Total Fat . . . . 1 g
   Saturated Fat . . . . . . 0 g
Cholesterol . . . . 3 mg
Sodium . . . . 173 mg
Carbohydrate . . . . . . 26 g
   Dietary Fiber . . . . . . 6 g
   Sugars . . . . 21 g
Protein . . . . 2 g

Cantaloupe Salad

Preparation time: 15 minutes
Serves 6   Serving size: 1 slice

1 cup reduced-fat whipped topping

3 Tbsp frozen orange juice concentrate, thawed and undiluted

1 medium cantaloupe

Lettuce leaves

1 cup seedless green grapes, halved

1. Combine the whipped topping and orange juice, mixing well.

2. Cut the cantaloupe into 6 sections, removing the seeds and peel. Place the cantaloupe on lettuce leaves; spoon grapes over and around each section.

3. Drizzle with the whipped topping mixture and serve.

Exchanges
1 Fruit
1/2 Fat

Calories 92
  Calories from Fat . . 16
Total Fat . . . . 2 g
  Saturated Fat . . . . . . 1 g
Cholesterol . . . . 0 mg
Sodium . . . . 12 mg
Carbohydrate . . . . . . 18 g
  Dietary Fiber . . . . . . 1 g
  Sugars . . . . 15 g
Protein . . . . 1 g

Chicken Salad

Preparation time: 15 minutes
Serves 6   Serving size: 1/2 cup

4 boneless, skinless chicken breast halves, cooked and cubed
1/3 cup reduced-fat mayonnaise
2 Tbsp cider vinegar
3/4 cup chopped celery
6 stalks green onion, chopped
1/2 cup chopped pecans
1/8 tsp garlic powder
1/4 tsp salt
1/8 tsp pepper
   Lettuce leaves

1. Combine all ingredients except the lettuce in a medium bowl and mix well.

2. Refrigerate until serving time. Serve on a bed of lettuce.

Exchanges
1/2 Starch
2 Very Lean Meat
2 Monounsaturated Fat

Calories 213
   Calories from Fat . 113
Total Fat . . . . 13 g
   Saturated Fat . . . . . . 1 g
Cholesterol . . . . 53 mg
Sodium . . . . 236 mg
Carbohydrate . . . . 6 g
   Dietary Fiber . . . . . . 2 g
   Sugars . . . . 2 g
Protein . . . . 19 g

CJ's California Taco Salad

Preparation time: 20 minutes
Serves 12   Serving size: 1 salad

1 1/2 lb lean ground beef
1 pkg taco seasoning mix
6 oz mild salsa
1/2 cup water
12 oz baked tortilla chips
1 medium head lettuce, shredded
3 large tomatoes, seeded and chopped
6 oz fat-free sour cream
6 oz reduced-fat shredded cheddar cheese

1. Brown the beef in a nonstick skillet until it crumbles. Drain the fat from the beef. Add the taco seasoning, salsa, and water. Reduce the heat and simmer.

2. Layer the salad on 12 plates in this order: chips, meat, lettuce, tomato, sour cream, and cheese. Add taco sauce, if desired.

Exchanges
2 Starch
2 Medium-Fat Meat

Calories 302
   Calories from Fat . 107
Total Fat . . . . 12 g
   Saturated Fat . . . . . . 5 g
Cholesterol . . . . 45 mg
Sodium . . . . 575 mg
Carbohydrate . . . . . . 32 g
   Dietary Fiber . . . . . . 3 g
   Sugars . . . . 4 g
Protein . . . . 21 g

Creamy Salad Dressing

Preparation time: 5 minutes
Serves 8   Serving size: 1 Tbsp

   1/4 cup fat-free plain yogurt
   1/4 cup reduced-fat mayonnaise
    1 Tbsp chopped garlic
    2 tsp spicy brown mustard
    2 Tbsp honey

Combine all ingredients, mixing well. Chill before serving.

Exchanges
1/2 Carbohydrate

Calories 46
   Calories from Fat . . 21
Total Fat . . . . 2 g
   Saturated Fat . . . . . . 1 g
Cholesterol . . . . 3 mg
Sodium . . . . 67 mg
Carbohydrate . . . . 6 g
   Dietary Fiber . . . . . . 0 g
   Sugars . . . . 5 g
Protein . . . . 1 g

Fruit Salad

Preparation time: 20 minutes
Serves 12   Serving size: 1/2 cup

1 1/2	cups cubed cantaloupe
1 1/2	cups cubed honeydew melon
2	medium peaches, peeled and sliced
1	cup cubed fresh pineapple
1	cup grapes, halved
1	medium orange, peeled, seeded, and sliced
1	cup unsweetened Mandarin oranges
1	medium banana, sliced
16	oz fat-free sour cream
1/4	cup brown sugar
	Juice of 1 orange
	Juice of 1/2 lemon
3	Tbsp pineapple juice
1	tsp cinnamon

1. Combine the fruit except the banana in a large bowl and refrigerate.

2. Combine the remaining ingredients in a small bowl and mix well. Refrigerate.

3. To serve, add the bananas to the fruit. Toss with the dressing. Spoon in individual dishes.

Exchanges
1 1/2 Fruit

Calories 103
   Calories from Fat . . . 3
Total Fat . . . . 0 g
   Saturated Fat . . . . . . 0 g
Cholesterol . . . . 0 mg
Sodium . . . . 48 mg
Carbohydrate . . . . . . 24 g
   Dietary Fiber . . . . . . 2 g
   Sugars . . . . 20 g
Protein . . . . 2 g

Green Pea Salad

Preparation time: 10 minutes
Serves 6   Serving size: 1/2 cup

1/2 cup reduced-fat mayonnaise

1 tsp Dijon mustard

1 tsp vinegar

1/8 tsp salt

1/8 tsp pepper

2 16-oz pkg frozen green peas, thawed and drained

1 medium onion, finely chopped

2 eggs, boiled and chopped

1 tsp parsley

1. Combine the mayonnaise, mustard, vinegar, salt, and pepper in a small bowl and mix well.

2. Combine the peas, onion, and egg in a large bowl. Toss with the dressing and refrigerate. Sprinkle with parsley before serving.

Exchanges
1 1/2 Starch
2 Fat

Calories 206
   Calories from Fat . . 74
Total Fat . . . . 8 g
   Saturated Fat . . . . . . 2 g
Cholesterol . . . . 79 mg
Sodium . . . . 316 mg
Carbohydrate . . . . . . 24 g
   Dietary Fiber . . . . . . 8 g
   Sugars . . . . 10 g
Protein . . . . 9 g

Macaroni and Tuna Salad

Preparation time: 20 minutes
Serves 8   Serving size: 1/2 cup

8	oz uncooked macaroni noodles
1/2	cup reduced-fat mayonnaise
1/2	cup fat-free sour cream
2	tsp sugar
2	Tbsp cider vinegar
1	Tbsp prepared mustard
1 1/2	cups chopped celery
1/2	cup chopped onion
1/3	cup chopped green bell pepper
1	6-oz can water-packed tuna
1	egg, boiled and chopped
1/2	tsp salt
1/2	tsp pepper

1. Cook the macaroni according to package directions (but without adding salt), drain thoroughly, and rinse in cold water.

2. Combine the mayonnaise, sour cream, sugar, vinegar, and mustard in a small bowl and mix well.

3. Combine all ingredients in a large bowl and toss well. Chill before serving.

Exchanges
2 Starch
1 Lean Meat

Calories 217
  Calories from Fat . . 53
Total Fat . . . . 6 g
  Saturated Fat . . . . . . 1 g
Cholesterol . . . . 39 mg
Sodium . . . . 392 mg
Carbohydrate . . . . . . 29 g
  Dietary Fiber . . . . . . 1 g
  Sugars . . . . 6 g
Protein . . . . 11 g

Mango Mango Salad with Chicken

Preparation time: 20 minutes
Serves 6   Serving size: 1 cup

    1/3 cup reduced-fat mayonnaise
      3 stalks green onion, chopped
      2 cups cooked diced chicken
      2 cups chopped ripe mango
      1 green bell pepper, seeded and chopped
      2 Tbsp canola oil
      1 Tbsp apple cider vinegar
      1 Tbsp lemon juice
      1 tsp sugar
         Lettuce leaves

1. Combine the mayonnaise and green onion in a small bowl, cover, and chill. Combine the chicken, mango, and bell pepper in a large bowl.

2. Combine the oil, vinegar, lemon juice, and sugar in a container with a tight lid. Shake well. Add the mayonnaise and green onion and stir well.

3. Pour the dressing over salad, toss well, and chill for 30 minutes. To serve, spoon onto a plate lined with lettuce leaves.

Exchanges

1 Fruit	2 Fat
2 Very Lean Meat	

Calories 224
  Calories from Fat . 112
Total Fat . . . . 12 g
  Saturated Fat . . . . . . 3 g
Cholesterol . . . . 47 mg
Sodium . . . . 124 mg
Carbohydrate . . . . . . 14 g
  Dietary Fiber . . . . . . 2 g
  Sugars . . . . 11 g
Protein . . . . 14 g

Potato Salad with Dill

Preparation time: 20 minutes
Serves 8   Serving size: 1/2 cup

2	cups diced boiled potatoes
1/2	cup chopped celery
1/4	cup chopped onion
1/4	cup chopped green bell pepper
1	cup reduced-calorie mayonnaise
2	Tbsp prepared mustard
2	Tbsp apple cider vinegar
2	Tbsp pickle relish
1/2	tsp salt
1/2	tsp pepper
2	tsp dill

1. Combine the potatoes, celery, onion, and bell pepper in a large bowl.

2. Combine the mayonnaise, mustard, vinegar, pickle relish, salt, pepper, and dill in a medium bowl and mix well.

3. Toss the vegetables with the dressing and refrigerate before serving, allowing the flavors to blend.

Exchanges
1 Starch
1 1/2 Fat

Calories 146
  Calories from Fat . . 85
Total Fat . . . . 9 g
  Saturated Fat . . . . . . 2 g
Cholesterol . . . . 12 mg
Sodium . . . . 416 mg
Carbohydrate . . . . . . 14 g
  Dietary Fiber . . . . . . 1 g
  Sugars . . . . 4 g
Protein . . . . 1 g

Seafood Salad

Preparation time: 20 minutes
Serves 6   Serving size: 1/2 cup

- 1/2 cup reduced-calorie mayonnaise
- 1/3 cup fat-free Italian salad dressing
- 2 Tbsp Parmesan cheese
- 1 1/2 cups cooked blue crabmeat, flaked, shell pieces removed
- 2 cups cooked pasta, any shape
- 1 cup blanched broccoli flowerets
- 1/2 cup chopped green or red bell pepper
- 1 cup chopped tomatoes
- 1/3 cup chopped onion

1. Combine the mayonnaise, salad dressing, and cheese in a small bowl and mix well.

2. Combine the remaining ingredients in a large bowl. Add the dressing and toss. Chill before serving.

Exchanges
1 Starch
1 Vegetable
1 Very Lean Meat
1 Fat

Calories 189
  Calories from Fat . . 69
Total Fat . . . . 8 g
  Saturated Fat . . . . . . 2 g
Cholesterol . . . . 38 mg
Sodium . . . . 378 mg
Carbohydrate . . . . . . 20 g
  Dietary Fiber . . . . . . 2 g
  Sugars . . . . 5 g
Protein . . . . 10 g

Soul Slaw

Preparation time: 30 minutes
Serves 8   Serving size: 1 cup

1/2	cup reduced-fat mayonnaise
1/2	cup plain fat-free yogurt
1/4	cup apple cider vinegar
2	tsp sugar
2	Tbsp Dijon mustard
1/8	tsp salt
1	tsp celery seeds
	Pepper to taste
1	large head green cabbage, julienned
2	medium raw carrots, grated

1. Combine the mayonnaise, yogurt, vinegar, sugar, mustard, salt, celery seeds, and pepper in a small bowl and mix well.

2. Combine the cabbage and carrots in a large bowl. Add the dressing, toss well, and refrigerate for at least 1 hour before serving.

Exchanges
3 Vegetable
1 Fat

Calories 108
   Calories from Fat . . 46
Total Fat . . . . 5 g
   Saturated Fat . . . . . . 1 g
Cholesterol . . . . 6 mg
Sodium . . . . 216 mg
Carbohydrate . . . . . . 14 g
   Dietary Fiber . . . . . . 4 g
   Sugars . . . . 9 g
Protein . . . . 3 g

Appetizers

Celery with Shrimp

Preparation time: 15 minutes
Serves 16   Serving size: 1/2 stalk

1/2 lb cooked shrimp, chopped into chunky pieces

3 oz reduced-fat cream cheese, softened

2 Tbsp reduced-fat mayonnaise

1 Tbsp finely chopped onion

1 Tbsp finely chopped green bell pepper

1 Tbsp finely chopped green olive

Dash Worcestershire sauce

Dash hot pepper sauce

Salt to taste (optional)

Pepper to taste (optional)

8 celery stalks, cleaned, trimmed, and cut in half

Combine all ingredients and stuff the mixture diagonally into the celery stalks.

Exchanges
1 Very Lean Meat

Calories 37
   Calories from Fat . . 17
Total Fat . . . . 2 g
   Saturated Fat . . . . . . 1 g
Cholesterol . . . . 32 mg
Sodium . . . . 84 mg
Carbohydrate . . . . 1 g
   Dietary Fiber . . . . . . 0 g
   Sugars . . . . 1 g
Protein . . . . 4 g

Chicken Puffs

Preparation time: 30 minutes
Serves 12   Serving size: 1 puff

1/4 cup boiling water

2 Tbsp margarine

1/4 cup flour

1/8 tsp salt

1/4 cup egg substitute

1/4 cup grated Swiss cheese

2 cups cooked chopped chicken

2 Tbsp chopped pimiento

2 Tbsp white wine

1/4 cup reduced-fat mayonnaise

1. Heat the oven to 400 degrees. Boil the water in a medium saucepan. Melt the margarine in the boiling water. Stir in the flour and salt.

2. Cook over medium heat, stirring vigorously, until the mixture forms a ball. Remove from the heat and let cool.

3. Add the egg substitute and beat for 1 minute. Drop the mixture by teaspoonfuls on a nonstick cookie sheet and bake for 20 minutes. Remove from the oven.

4. Combine the remaining ingredients and stuff the puff shells with the chicken salad mixture.

Exchanges
1 Medium-Fat Meat
1/2 Fat

Calories 100
    Calories from Fat . . 50
Total Fat . . . . 6 g
    Saturated Fat . . . . . . 2 g
Cholesterol . . . . 25 mg
Sodium . . . . 106 mg
Carbohydrate . . . . 3 g
    Dietary Fiber . . . . . . 0 g
    Sugars . . . . 0 g
Protein . . . . 8 g

Cranberry-Lemon Relish

Preparation time: 10 minutes
Serves 8   Serving size: 1/4 cup

- 2 cups cranberries
- 1 large red apple, diced
- 1 small lemon, unpeeled, quartered, and seeded
- 1/2 cup sugar
- 1/4 tsp nutmeg
- 1/4 tsp cinnamon
- 1/4 tsp mace

1. Chop the cranberries, apple, and lemon in a blender or food processor just until chunky. Do not overblend.

2. Add the sugar and spices and stir until the sugar is dissolved. Chill before serving.

Exchanges
1 1/2 Carbohydrate

Calories 79
   Calories from Fat . . . 2
Total Fat . . . . 0 g
   Saturated Fat . . . . . . 0 g
Cholesterol . . . . 0 mg
Sodium . . . . 1 mg
Carbohydrate . . . . . . 22 g
   Dietary Fiber . . . . . . 2 g
   Sugars . . . . 18 g
Protein . . . . 0 g

Golden Party Punch

Preparation time: 15 minutes
Serves 8   Serving size: 1 cup

3 oz orange-flavored, sugar-free gelatin

1 cup boiling water

6 oz canned frozen orange juice concentrate

2 cups pineapple juice

2 cups apple juice

12 oz diet ginger ale

1. Dissolve the gelatin in the boiling water. Mix in frozen concentrate and juices.

2. Stir in the ginger ale just before serving.

Exchanges
1 1/2 Fruit

Calories 102
  Calories from Fat . . . 1
Total Fat . . . . 0 g
  Saturated Fat . . . . . . 0 g
Cholesterol . . . . 0 mg
Sodium . . . . 34 mg
Carbohydrate . . . . . . 24 g
  Dietary Fiber . . . . . . 0 g
  Sugars . . . . 23 g
Protein . . . . 1 g

Ham Roll

Preparation time: 15 minutes
Serves 8   Serving size: 1 ham roll

> 8 oz reduced-fat cream cheese, softened
>
> 2 Tbsp fat-free (skim) milk
>
> 1 Tbsp finely chopped parsley
>
> 8 thin slices boiled ham (about 1 lb)
>
> 1 16-oz jar pickled okra

1. Whip the cream cheese and milk in a blender or food processor until fluffy. Add the parsley.

2. Spread each ham slice with 1 oz of the cream cheese mixture. Place some pickled okra in the center of each slice and roll it up. Slice each ham roll in half to serve.

Exchanges
1 Medium-Fat Meat

Calories 67
   Calories from Fat . . 41
Total Fat . . . . 5 g
   Saturated Fat . . . . . . 3 g
Cholesterol . . . . 18 mg
Sodium . . . . 337 mg
Carbohydrate . . . . 2 g
   Dietary Fiber . . . . . . 1 g
   Sugars . . . . 1 g
Protein . . . . 4 g

Party Meatballs

Preparation time: 30 minutes
Serves 8   Serving size: 3 meatballs

   1   lb extra-lean (95% fat-free) ground beef
  1/2 cup breadcrumbs
  1/4 cup egg substitute
   1   medium onion, finely chopped
   1   Tbsp parsley
   1   tsp Worcestershire sauce
  1/4 cup fat-free (skim) milk
       Salt to taste (optional)
       Pepper to taste (optional)
   2   tsp canola oil
  1/4 cup reduced-fat, reduced-sodium chicken broth
 1 1/4 cups reduced-calorie grape jelly or preserves
  1/4 cup catsup

1. Mix the ground beef, breadcrumbs, egg substitute, onion, parsley, Worcestershire sauce, milk, salt, and pepper together in a large bowl.

2. Roll into 24 1-inch balls. Heat the oil in a large skillet and brown the meatballs over medium heat. Stir in the chicken broth.

3. Meanwhile, melt the grape jelly or preserves and catsup together in a small saucepan over low heat until hot and pour over the meatballs. Cook for 30 minutes.

Exchanges
1 1/2 Carbohydrate
2 Very Lean Meat

Calories 191
  Calories from Fat . . 36
Total Fat . . . . 4 g
  Saturated Fat . . . . . . 0 g
Cholesterol . . . . 34 mg
Sodium . . . . 235 mg
Carbohydrate . . . . . . 23 g
  Dietary Fiber . . . . . . 1 g
  Sugars . . . . 9 g
Protein . . . . 14 g

Salmon Party Log

Preparation time: 20 minutes
Serves 8   Serving size: 1 slice

16 oz canned pink salmon, bones and skin removed, well drained

1 Tbsp lemon juice

1 tsp prepared horseradish

1/8 tsp liquid smoke seasoning (optional)

8 oz fat-free cream cheese, softened

2 Tbsp fat-free (skim) milk

2 tsp minced onion

1/4 tsp salt

1/2 cup finely chopped pecans

3 Tbsp chopped fresh parsley

1. Stir together the salmon, lemon juice, horseradish, liquid smoke (if desired), cream cheese, milk, onion, and salt. Cover and chill for 2 hours.

2. Shape the mixture into a 7-inch log. Stir the pecans and parsley together in a shallow dish.

3. Roll the log in the pecan mixture, wrap in plastic wrap, and chill. Serve with assorted crackers.

Exchanges
2 Medium-Fat Meat

Calories 154
Calories from Fat . . 74
Total Fat . . . . 8 g
Saturated Fat . . . . . . 0 g
Cholesterol . . . . 35 mg
Sodium . . . . 543 mg
Carbohydrate . . . . 4 g
Dietary Fiber . . . . . . 1 g
Sugars . . . . 1 g
Protein . . . . 16 g

Salmon Spread

Preparation time: 15 minutes
Serves 16   Serving size: 1 Tbsp

16 oz canned salmon, skin and bones removed, well drained

8 oz reduced-fat cream cheese, softened

1 Tbsp lemon juice

3 Tbsp grated onion

1 tsp liquid smoke seasoning

1/2 tsp mustard

1/2 tsp salt

2 Tbsp chopped fresh parsley

Flake the salmon and combine it with all the ingredients. Chill before serving with your favorite crackers.

Exchanges
1 Medium-Fat Meat

Calories 75
    Calories from Fat . . 42
Total Fat . . . . 5 g
    Saturated Fat . . . . . . 2 g
Cholesterol . . . . 26 mg
Sodium . . . . 290 mg
Carbohydrate . . . . 1 g
    Dietary Fiber . . . . . . 0 g
    Sugars . . . . 1 g
Protein . . . . 7 g

Shrimp Dip

Preparation time: 15 minutes
Serves 16   Serving size: 1 Tbsp

2 Tbsp catsup

8 oz fat-free cream cheese, softened

1/2 cup minced onion

2 Tbsp reduced-fat mayonnaise

1 Tbsp lemon juice

1 tsp Worcestershire sauce

1 lb shelled, cooked shrimp, diced

3 sprigs fresh dill

1. Mix the catsup, cream cheese, onion, mayonnaise, lemon juice, and Worcestershire sauce together until well blended.

2. Add the shrimp and stir. Garnish with fresh dill and serve with low-sodium crackers.

Exchanges
1 Lean Meat

Calories 50
    Calories from Fat . . . 8
Total Fat . . . . 1 g
    Saturated Fat . . . . . . 0 g
Cholesterol . . . . 54 mg
Sodium . . . . 173 mg
Carbohydrate . . . . 2 g
    Dietary Fiber . . . . . . 0 g
    Sugars . . . . 1 g
Protein . . . . 8 g

Southern Spiced Tea

Preparation time: 10 minutes
Serves 8   Serving size: 1 cup

6 cups boiling water

3 Tbsp black tea

1 cinnamon stick

1 cup orange juice

2 Tbsp lemon juice

1/2 cup sugar

1. Pour the boiling water over the tea and cinnamon. Steep for 10 minutes.

2. Strain the tea and add the remaining ingredients. The tea can be served hot or cold.

Exchanges
1 Carbohydrate

Calories 63
   Calories from Fat . . . 0
Total Fat . . . . 0 g
   Saturated Fat . . . . . . 0 g
Cholesterol . . . . 0 mg
Sodium . . . . 1 mg
Carbohydrate . . . . . . 16 g
   Dietary Fiber . . . . . . 0 g
   Sugars . . . . 16 g
Protein . . . . 0 g

Spicy Shrimp Bites

Preparation time: 20 minutes
Serves 6   Serving size: 1/2 cup

1	lb medium-size raw shrimp, shelled and deveined
1	Tbsp rum
1/4	cup vinegar
2	Tbsp lite soy sauce
4	tsp sugar
2	tsp cornstarch
2	Tbsp canola oil
3	cloves garlic, minced
1/4	tsp red pepper flakes
1 1/2	Tbsp fresh minced ginger

1. Toss the shrimp with the rum. Combine the vinegar, soy sauce, sugar, and cornstarch in a small bowl and mix well.

2. Heat the canola oil in a wok or large skillet. When the oil gets hot, add the garlic, red pepper flakes, and ginger.

3. Add the shrimp and cook for 3 minutes until the sauce bubbles and thickens. Serve with toothpicks.

Exchanges
1/2 Carbohydrate
1 Medium-Fat Meat

Calories 114
  Calories from Fat . . 47
Total Fat . . . . 5 g
  Saturated Fat . . . . . . 0 g
Cholesterol . . . . 84 mg
Sodium . . . . 311 mg
Carbohydrate . . . . 6 g
  Dietary Fiber . . . . . . 1 g
  Sugars . . . . 5 g
Protein . . . . 10 g

Strawberry Smoothie

Preparation time: 15 minutes
Serves 5   Serving size: 1 cup

3 cups cranberry juice cocktail

8 oz reduced-fat vanilla yogurt

1 pint fresh strawberries, cleaned, tops removed

1 banana, sliced

1. Combine half of all ingredients in a blender or food processor, and blend or process until smooth.

2. Repeat with the remaining ingredients. Combine the mixtures together and pour into individual glasses to serve.

Exchanges
3 Fruit

Calories 174
  Calories from Fat . . 10
Total Fat . . . . 1 g
  Saturated Fat . . . . . . 0 g
Cholesterol . . . . 4 mg
Sodium . . . . 32 mg
Carbohydrate . . . . . . 40 g
  Dietary Fiber . . . . . . 2 g
  Sugars . . . . 35 g
Protein . . . . 3 g

Stuffed Strawberries

Preparation time: 20 minutes
Serves 20   Serving size: 1 strawberry

20	large fresh strawberries
3	oz fat-free cream cheese, softened
1	Tbsp fat-free (skim) milk
1	Tbsp finely chopped pecans
1 1/2	Tbsp powdered sugar
1	tsp almond liqueur

1. Dice 2 strawberries horizontally and set aside. Cut a thin slice from the stem end of each remaining strawberry, forming a base for the strawberry to stand on.

2. Cut each strawberry into four wedges starting at the pointed end. Be careful to cut to, but not through, the stem end.

3. Beat the cream cheese and milk at medium speed with an electric mixer until fluffy. Stir in the diced strawberries, pecans, powdered sugar, and almond liqueur.

4. Spoon about 1 tsp of the mixture into each strawberry. You can prepare the stuffing up to a day ahead, but do not stuff the strawberries more than 4 hours before serving.

Exchanges
Free

Calories 17
  Calories from Fat . . . 3
Total Fat . . . . 0 g
  Saturated Fat . . . . . . 0 g
Cholesterol . . . . 1 mg
Sodium . . . . 24 mg
Carbohydrate . . . . 3 g
  Dietary Fiber . . . . . . 1 g
  Sugars . . . . 2 g
Protein . . . . 1 g

Tangy Shrimp Dip

Preparation time: 15 minutes
Serves 16   Serving size: 1 Tbsp

- 12 oz small curd, reduced-fat cottage cheese
- 1/4 cup reduced-fat mayonnaise
- 2 Tbsp chili sauce
- 1 Tbsp lemon juice
- 5 oz canned tiny shrimp, drained and well rinsed
- 2 Tbsp diced onion
- Salt to taste (optional)
- Pepper to taste (optional)

1. Combine the cottage cheese, mayonnaise, chili sauce, and lemon juice. Beat until smooth.

2. Stir in the remaining ingredients. Chill thoroughly and serve with assorted crackers.

Exchanges
1 Lean Meat

Calories 45
Calories from Fat . . 15
Total Fat . . . . 2 g
Saturated Fat . . . . . . 1 g
Cholesterol . . . . 19 mg
Sodium . . . . 148 mg
Carbohydrate . . . . . . 2 g
Dietary Fiber . . . . . . 0 g
Sugars . . . . 1 g
Protein . . . . 5 g

Tuna Ball

Preparation time: 15 minutes
Serves 8   Serving size: 1/8 recipe

> 2   6 1/2-oz cans water-packed tuna, well drained
>
> 8   oz reduced-fat cream cheese, softened
>
> 1   Tbsp pickle relish, drained
>
> 1   Tbsp finely chopped onion
>
> 1/2   cup chopped fresh parsley

1. Combine the tuna, cream cheese, relish, and onion in a bowl and mix until cream cheese is slightly chunky.

2. Form the mixture into a ball. Roll the ball in the parsley and chill before serving. Serve with pita bread wedges.

Exchanges
2 Lean Meat

Calories 122
  Calories from Fat . . 57
Total Fat . . . . 6 g
  Saturated Fat . . . . . . 4 g
Cholesterol . . . . 32 mg
Sodium . . . . 280 mg
Carbohydrate . . . . 2 g
  Dietary Fiber . . . . . . 0 g
  Sugars . . . . 2 g
Protein . . . . 14 g

Desserts

Apple and Blueberry Tart

Preparation time: 20 minutes
Serves 8   Serving size: 1 slice

1/2	lb frozen puff pastry, thawed
4	green apples, peeled and cut into 1/4-inch slices
1	cup fresh or frozen blueberries
2	Tbsp lemon juice
1/3	cup brown sugar
2	Tbsp flour
3/4	tsp cinnamon
1	Tbsp reduced-fat margarine

1. Roll out the pastry to a 14-inch circle and lightly flour the surface. Transfer to large cookie sheet and chill.

2. Heat the oven to 350 degrees. Place the fruit in a bowl and toss with the lemon juice. Add the sugar, flour, and cinnamon and mix well. Arrange the fruit in the center of the pastry, leaving a 2-inch border. Cut the margarine into bits over the fruit.

3. Fold the edge of the pastry up and over the fruit, overlapping to form the sides. Brush the folds with water and pinch to seal. Bake for 20–30 minutes. If the tart browns too quickly, cover with foil. Cool 10 minutes and serve.

Exchanges
2 1/2 Carbohydrate
1 1/2 Fat

Calories 238
   Calories from Fat . . 78
Total Fat . . . . 9 g
   Saturated Fat . . . . . . 2 g
Cholesterol . . . . 0 mg
Sodium . . . . 111 mg
Carbohydrate . . . . . . 40 g
   Dietary Fiber . . . . . . 4 g
   Sugars . . . . 20 g
Protein . . . . 3 g

Apple Crisp

Preparation time: 20 minutes
Serves 6   Serving size: 1/2 cup

    4 large baking apples, peeled and sliced
  3/4 cup brown sugar
  1/2 cup flour
  3/4 cup oatmeal
  3/4 tsp cinnamon
  3/4 tsp nutmeg
  1/3 cup reduced-fat margarine

1. Heat the oven to 350 degrees. Spray a baking pan with nonstick cooking spray and place the apples in the pan.

2. Mix the brown sugar, flour, oatmeal, cinnamon, and nutmeg together and place on top of the apple. Drop dots of margarine over the dry mixture. Bake for 25 minutes.

Exchanges
4 Carbohydrate
1 Fat

Calories 298
   Calories from Fat . . 55
Total Fat . . . . 6 g
   Saturated Fat . . . . . . 1 g
Cholesterol . . . . 0 mg
Sodium . . . . 91 mg
Carbohydrate . . . . . . 61 g
   Dietary Fiber . . . . . . 4 g
   Sugars . . . . 44 g
Protein . . . . 3 g

Aunt Dorothy's Tea Cakes

Preparation time: 20 minutes
Serves 12   Serving size: 1 tea cake

1/2 cup reduced-fat margarine

3/4 cup sugar

1/2 cup egg substitute

1/2 cup low-fat buttermilk

1/4 cup molasses

　2 cups flour

1/2 tsp baking soda

　1 tsp baking powder

1/2 tsp nutmeg

1. Heat the oven to 375 degrees. Cream the margarine and sugar together. Add 1/4 cup of egg substitute and mix well, then another 1/4 cup and mix well.

2. Combine the milk and molasses. In a separate bowl, combine the dry ingredients. Alternately add milk and flour portions to the margarine mixture until all the portions are added.

3. Drop the batter by spoonfuls onto a nonstick baking sheet. Bake for 12–15 minutes.

Exchanges
2 1/2 Carbohydrate
1/2 Fat

Calories 187
　Calories from Fat . . 36
Total Fat . . . . 4 g
　Saturated Fat . . . . . . 1 g
Cholesterol . . . . 0 mg
Sodium . . . . 175 mg
Carbohydrate . . . . . . 34 g
　Dietary Fiber . . . . . . 1 g
　Sugars . . . . 18 g
Protein . . . . 4 g

Baked Apples

Preparation time: 20 minutes
Serves 6   Serving size: 1 apple

> 6 medium baking apples
> 1/4 cup boiling water
> 1/3 cup sugar
>   1 tsp cinnamon
>   2 Tbsp reduced-fat margarine

1. Heat the oven to 350 degrees. Wash and core the apples, but do not peel them. Place the apples in a nonstick baking dish.

2. Add the water to the apples. Mix the sugar and cinnamon together and spoon into the cavity of the apples. Add margarine to each cavity.

3. Cover and bake for 30 minutes or until the apples are tender. Serve hot.

Exchanges
2 Carbohydrate
1/2 Fat

Calories 152
    Calories from Fat . . 22
Total Fat . . . . 2 g
    Saturated Fat . . . . . . 0 g
Cholesterol . . . . 0 mg
Sodium . . . . 30 mg
Carbohydrate . . . . . . 35 g
    Dietary Fiber . . . . . . 4 g
    Sugars . . . . 31 g
Protein . . . . 0 g

Bananas Foster

Preparation time: 15 minutes
Serves 4   Serving size: 1 banana

>   2 Tbsp reduced-fat margarine
>   4 small bananas
>   2 Tbsp brown sugar
>   Dash ground cinnamon
>   1 Tbsp banana liqueur
> 1/2 cup fat-free, sugar-free, rum-flavored ice cream

1. Melt the margarine in a small skillet. Cut the bananas in half and brown in the margarine.

2. Sprinkle the bananas with the brown sugar, cinnamon, and liqueur and set aflame. Serve blazing with ice cream.

Exchanges
2 Carbohydrate
1/2 Fat

Calories 145
  Calories from Fat . . 28
Total Fat . . . . 3 g
  Saturated Fat . . . . . . 1 g
Cholesterol . . . . 0 mg
Sodium . . . . 68 mg
Carbohydrate . . . . . . 30 g
  Dietary Fiber . . . . . . 2 g
  Sugars . . . . 21 g
Protein . . . . 2 g

Bread Pudding

Preparation time: 20 minutes
Serves 8   Serving size: 1/2 cup

1/2 cup raisins

6 cups whole-wheat bread, cubed

1 16-oz can peaches packed in their own juice, drained

1 cup sugar

2 tsp vanilla

2 tsp butter-flavored extract

1 cup egg substitute

2 13-oz cans evaporated fat-free (skim) milk plus water to make 4 cups

1 tsp cinnamon

1 tsp nutmeg

1 tsp lemon juice

1. Heat the oven to 350 degrees. Layer the raisins, bread, and peaches in a 3-quart nonstick baking dish (or spray the dish with nonstick cooking spray).

2. Beat the remaining ingredients together and pour the mixture over the bread and peaches. Place the dish in a hot water bath and bake for 45 minutes or until a toothpick inserted in the center comes out clean.

Exchanges
4 Carbohydrate

Calories 283
 Calories from Fat . . 10
Total Fat . . . . 1 g
 Saturated Fat . . . . . . 0 g
Cholesterol . . . . 3 mg
Sodium . . . . 274 mg
Carbohydrate . . . . . . 58 g
 Dietary Fiber . . . . . . 2 g
 Sugars . . . . 45 g
Protein . . . . 13 g

Candace's Fruit Delight

Preparation time: 20 minutes
Serves 6   Serving size: 3/4 cup

2	Tbsp honey
3	Tbsp lemon juice
1 1/4	tsp cinnamon
2 1/2	cups bite-sized watermelon pieces
1/2	cup orange sections
1	cup sliced strawberries
1/2	cup halved seedless grapes

1. Combine the honey, lemon juice, and cinnamon in a small bowl and mix well. Chill until cold.

2. Combine the fruit and toss with the dressing. Serve on a bed of lettuce.

Exchanges
1 Fruit

Calories 67
   Calories from Fat . . . 4
Total Fat . . . . 0 g
   Saturated Fat . . . . . . 0 g
Cholesterol . . . . 0 mg
Sodium . . . . 4 mg
Carbohydrate . . . . . . 17 g
   Dietary Fiber . . . . . . 1 g
   Sugars . . . . 15 g
Protein . . . . 1 g

Cheesecake Tarts

Preparation time: 20 minutes
Serves 10   Serving size: 1 tart

> 2   8-oz pkg fat-free cream cheese, softened
> 1/2   cup sugar
> 1   cup egg substitute
> 1   tsp vanilla
> 2   tsp lemon juice
> 10   vanilla wafers

1. Heat the oven to 350 degrees. Whip the cream cheese for 2 minutes or until fluffy. Add the sugar, egg substitute, vanilla, and lemon juice. Mix well.

2. Place 10 aluminum cupcake holders in muffin tins and add water to the 2 empty holes in tin. Place a vanilla wafer in the bottom of each holder and pour the batter over each vanilla wafer.

3. Bake for 20 minutes. Remove from the heat and cool. If desired, top each tart with 1 tsp of jam or jelly (not included in nutritional analysis).

Exchanges
1 1/2 Carbohydrate

Calories 116
  Calories from Fat . . . 6
Total Fat . . . . 1 g
  Saturated Fat . . . . . . 0 g
Cholesterol . . . . 8 mg
Sodium . . . . 311 mg
Carbohydrate . . . . . . 17 g
  Dietary Fiber . . . . . . 0 g
  Sugars . . . . 13 g
Protein . . . . 10 g

Fruit Cup

Preparation time: 20 minutes
Serves 2   Serving size: 3/4 cup

> 1/2 cup honeydew balls
>
> 1/2 cup cantaloupe balls
>
> 1/2 cup halved fresh strawberries
>
>   3 Tbsp orange liqueur
>
>   Fresh mint leaves

1. Combine all the ingredients except the mint. Toss gently to coat. Cover and chill for 2 hours.

2. Spoon into individual compote dishes and garnish with mint leaves to serve.

Exchanges
2 Carbohydrate

Calories 128
   Calories from Fat . . . 3
Total Fat . . . . 0 g
   Saturated Fat . . . . . . 0 g
Cholesterol . . . . 0 mg
Sodium . . . . 10 mg
Carbohydrate . . . . . . 22 g
   Dietary Fiber . . . . . . 1 g
   Sugars . . . . 21 g
Protein . . . . 1 g

Jeanette's Custard

Preparation time: 10 minutes
Serves 4   Serving size: 1/2 cup

2 eggs
3 Tbsp sugar
1 tsp vanilla
1 2/3 cups fat-free (skim) milk
1/2 tsp nutmeg

1. Heat the oven to 325 degrees. Combine the eggs, sugar, vanilla, and milk in a medium bowl. Beat well and pour into individual custard cups or a baking dish.

2. Sprinkle nutmeg over the mixture and bake for 35 minutes. The custard is done when a knife inserted in the center of the custard comes out clean.

Exchanges
1 Carbohydrate
1/2 Fat

Calories 109
   Calories from Fat . . 24
Total Fat . . . . 3 g
   Saturated Fat . . . . . . 1 g
Cholesterol . . . . 108 mg
Sodium . . . . 84 mg
Carbohydrate . . . . . . 15 g
   Dietary Fiber . . . . . . 0 g
   Sugars . . . . 14 g
Protein . . . . 7 g

Key Lime Pie

Preparation time: 20 minutes
Serves 8   Serving size: 1 slice

1 3/4 cups graham cracker crumbs

4 Tbsp reduced-fat margarine

3 eggs, separated

1 12-oz can evaporated fat-free (skim) milk

1 Tbsp cornstarch

1/3 cup sugar

1/3 cup fresh key lime juice

3 drops green food coloring

1/4 cup sugar

1. Preheat the oven to 350 degrees. Combine the graham cracker crumbs and margarine in a medium bowl and cut to mix. Press into a 9-inch pie pan and bake for 7–10 minutes or until browned.

2. Combine egg yolks, milk, cornstarch, and 1/3 cup sugar in a saucepan. Cook over medium heat, bringing the mixture to a boil. Remove from the heat and add the lime juice and the food coloring. Pour the mixture into the crust.

3. Beat the egg whites with a mixer until peaks form. Add 1/4 cup sugar and beat until stiff.

4. Spoon the meringue over the filling and bake until the edges are lightly brown, about 2–3 minutes. Cool before serving.

Exchanges
2 1/2 Carbohydrate
1 Fat

Calories 222
  Calories from Fat . . 53
Total Fat . . . . 6 g
  Saturated Fat . . . . . . 2 g
Cholesterol . . . . 82 mg
Sodium . . . . 224 mg
Carbohydrate . . . . . . 35 g
  Dietary Fiber . . . . . . 1 g
  Sugars . . . . 23 g
Protein . . . . 7 g

Pineapple Upside-Down Cake

Preparation time: 20 minutes
Serves 8   Serving size: 1 piece

          8 pineapple rings packed in their own juice
          2 Tbsp molasses
        1/3 cup reduced-fat margarine
        1/2 cup honey
          2 egg whites
     1 1/2 cups flour
        1/2 tsp baking soda
        3/4 cup pineapple juice (use the juice from the pineapple
              rings, and add water if necessary)

1. Heat the oven to 350 degrees. Spray a 9-inch baking pan with nonstick cooking spray. Arrange the pineapple rings on the bottom of the pan. Pour the molasses over the pineapple.

2. In a separate bowl, beat the margarine, honey, and egg whites. Add the remaining ingredients and stir until smooth. Pour the batter over the pineapple.

3. Bake for 30–35 minutes. Cool before serving.

Exchanges
3 Carbohydrate
1/2 Fat

Calories 237
    Calories from Fat . . 36
Total Fat . . . . 4 g
    Saturated Fat . . . . . . 1 g
Cholesterol . . . . 0 mg
Sodium . . . . 156 mg
Carbohydrate . . . . . . 48 g
    Dietary Fiber . . . . . . 1 g
    Sugars . . . . 29 g
Protein . . . . 4 g

Red Velvet Cake

Preparation time: 30 minutes
Serves 10   Serving size: 1 square

1/2	cup	shortening
1	cup	sugar
1	cup	egg substitute
2	Tbsp	cocoa
1 1/2	Tbsp	red food coloring
1	tsp	vanilla
2 1/2	cups	flour
1/2	tsp	salt
1	tsp	baking soda
1	cup	low-fat (1%) buttermilk
1	Tbsp	vinegar
1	cup	reduced-fat whipped topping

1. Heat the oven to 350 degrees. Cream the shortening, sugar, and egg substitute together. In a small bowl, make a thick paste of the cocoa and food coloring and add it to the cream mixture. Stir in the vanilla.

2. Sift together the flour, salt, and baking soda. Alternately add portions of the flour mixture and the buttermilk to the creamed mixture, stirring well.

3. Mix in the vinegar and pour the batter into a 9 × 9-inch or oblong pan. Bake for 30 minutes. Allow to cool. Cut into 10 squares and top each square with whipped topping.

Exchanges
3 Carbohydrate
2 Fat

Calories 326
  Calories from Fat . 106
Total Fat . . . . 12 g
  Saturated Fat . . . . . . 3 g
Cholesterol . . . . 1 mg
Sodium . . . . 314 mg
Carbohydrate . . . . . . 48 g
  Dietary Fiber . . . . . . 1 g
  Sugars . . . . 23 g
Protein . . . . 7 g

Rice Pudding

Preparation time: 20 minutes
Serves 10   Serving size: 1/2 cup

> 1 1/2 cups cooked rice
> 3/4 cup raisins
> 1/2 cup sugar
> 2 eggs
> 3/4 cup egg substitute
> 1 tsp vanilla
> 1 tsp cinnamon
> Dash nutmeg
> 2 cups fat-free (skim) milk, scalded
> 2 tsp melted reduced-fat margarine

1. Heat the oven to 350 degrees. Combine the rice, raisins, sugar, eggs, egg substitute, vanilla, cinnamon, and nutmeg in a large bowl.

2. Add the milk and margarine and mix well. Pour the batter into a 1 1/2-quart casserole.

3. Place the casserole in a hot water bath and bake for 1 hour or until the pudding is firm.

Exchanges
2 Carbohydrate

Calories 148
   Calories from Fat . . 14
Total Fat . . . . 2 g
   Saturated Fat . . . . . . 0 g
Cholesterol . . . . 43 mg
Sodium . . . . 78 mg
Carbohydrate . . . . . . 28 g
   Dietary Fiber . . . . . . 1 g
   Sugars . . . . 20 g
Protein . . . . 6 g

Skillet Peach Upside-Down Cake

Preparation time: 25 minutes
Serves 10   Serving size: 1 slice

1/3	cup reduced-fat margarine
1/2	cup brown sugar
1/2	cup sugar
1	16-oz can sliced peaches, packed in their own juice
4	maraschino cherries, sliced
1	cup egg substitute
2/3	cup fat-free (skim) milk
1 1/2	cups flour
3	tsp baking powder
1/8	tsp salt

1. Heat the oven to 350 degrees. Melt the margarine and sugars in a small saucepan until the sugar is dissolved. Remove from the heat.

2. Drain the peaches and place them in the center of a heavy ovenproof skillet or 9-inch cake pan, forming a circle. Sprinkle the cherries on top.

3. Add the egg and milk to the sugar mixture. In a separate bowl, combine the flour, baking powder, and salt. Add the flour in increments to the sugar mixture and mix well.

4. Pour the batter over the peaches and bake for 40 minutes.

Exchanges
3 Carbohydrate

Calories	215
Calories from Fat	29
Total Fat	3 g
Saturated Fat	1 g
Cholesterol	0 mg
Sodium	189 mg
Carbohydrate	42 g
Dietary Fiber	1 g
Sugars	27 g
Protein	5 g

Sponge Cake

Preparation time: 20 minutes
Serves 12   Serving size: 1 slice

7	egg whites and yolks
1 1/4	cups sugar
1/3	cup fat-free (skim) milk, scalded, slightly cooled
1	tsp vanilla
1	Tbsp lemon juice
1	cup cake flour

1. Heat the oven to 350 degrees. Beat the egg whites until stiff. In a separate bowl, mix the egg yolk and sugar until the mixture is creamy and lemon-colored.

2. Add the milk, vanilla, and lemon juice to the egg yolk mixture and beat well. Fold the flour by spoonfuls into the mixture. Fold in the egg whites.

3. Bake for 40 minutes or until the cake springs back to the touch.

Exchanges
2 Carbohydrate
1/2 Fat

Calories 168
  Calories from Fat . . 27
Total Fat . . . . 3 g
  Saturated Fat . . . . . . 1 g
Cholesterol . . . . 124 mg
Sodium . . . . 41 mg
Carbohydrate . . . . . . 31 g
  Dietary Fiber . . . . . . 0 g
  Sugars . . . . 22 g
Protein . . . . 5 g

Strawberry Cake

Preparation time: 15 minutes
Serves 6   Serving size: 1/2 cup

6	ladyfingers or 1 small sponge cake
1 1/4	cup sliced fresh strawberries
3	Tbsp sugar
1/2	tsp vanilla
1/3	cup reduced-fat whipped topping
1	Tbsp chopped walnuts

1. Line a medium glass dish with split ladyfingers or sliced sponge cake. In a small bowl, toss the strawberries with the sugar.

2. In a separate bowl, add the vanilla to the whipped topping. Sprinkle some berries over the cake, then add a layer of whipped topping. Sprinkle with nuts.

3. Repeat in layers until all ingredients are used, ending with a layer of whipped topping and nuts.

Exchanges
1 Carbohydrate
1/2 Fat

Calories 97
   Calories from Fat . . 20
Total Fat . . . . 2 g
   Saturated Fat . . . . . . 0 g
Cholesterol . . . . 47 mg
Sodium . . . . 20 mg
Carbohydrate . . . . . . 18 g
   Dietary Fiber . . . . . . 1 g
   Sugars . . . . 13 g
Protein . . . . 1 g

Strawberry Cream

Preparation time: 15 minutes
Serves 8   Serving size: 1/2 cup

> 2   3-oz pkg sugar-free strawberry-flavored gelatin
>
> 2   cups boiling water
>
> 12   oz sugar-free lemon-lime soda
>
> 2   cups reduced-fat whipped topping

1. Dissolve the gelatin in the boiling water. Stir in the soda and chill until almost firm.

2. Whip the mixture until foamy and fold in whipped topping. Place the mixture into a large glass bowl or individual serving dishes and chill until firm.

Exchanges
1/2 Carbohydrate
1/2 Saturated Fat

Calories 48
  Calories from Fat . . 18
Total Fat . . . . 2 g
  Saturated Fat . . . . . . 2 g
Cholesterol . . . . 0 mg
Sodium . . . . 63 mg
Carbohydrate . . . . 5 g
  Dietary Fiber . . . . . . 0 g
  Sugars . . . . 2 g
Protein . . . . 1 g

Sweet Potato Pie

Preparation time: 20 minutes
Serves 10   Serving size: 1 piece

3	large cooked sweet potatoes, peeled and mashed
3/4	cup sugar
1/2	cup egg substitute
2	tsp vanilla
1	tsp lemon-flavored extract
1	Tbsp butter-flavored extract
1	tsp cinnamon
1	tsp nutmeg
1/8	cup brandy
1	tsp lemon juice
1 1/2	cups evaporated fat-free (skim) milk
1	9-inch pie shell

1. Heat the oven to 350 degrees.

2. Mix all the ingredients together and beat until smooth. Pour into the pie shell and bake for 40 minutes.

Exchanges
3 1/2 Carbohydrate
1/2 Fat

Calories 270
   Calories from Fat . . 39
Total Fat . . . . 4 g
   Saturated Fat . . . . . . 1 g
Cholesterol . . . . 1 mg
Sodium . . . . 159 mg
Carbohydrate . . . . . . 52 g
   Dietary Fiber . . . . . . 3 g
   Sugars . . . . 31 g
Protein . . . . 7 g

Sweet Potato Pound Cake

Preparation time: 25 minutes
Serves 12   Serving size: 1 slice

> 1 cup reduced-fat margarine
> 1 cup sugar
> 1 cup brown sugar
> 2 1/2 cups cooked, mashed sweet potatoes
> 1 cup egg substitute
> 2 tsp vanilla
> 3 cups flour
> 1 tsp salt
> 1 tsp baking soda
> 2 tsp butter-flavored extract
> 1 tsp nutmeg
> 1 tsp cinnamon

1. Heat the oven to 350 degrees. Cream the margarine and sugars in a large bowl until fluffy. Add the sweet potatoes, egg, and vanilla and beat for 2 minutes.

2. Add the remaining ingredients and mix well. Pour the batter into a nonstick loaf pan and bake for 1 hour or until a toothpick inserted in the center comes out clean.

Exchanges
4 1/2 Carbohydrate
1 Fat

Calories 370
    Calories from Fat . . 70
Total Fat . . . . 8 g
    Saturated Fat . . . . . . 1 g
Cholesterol . . . . 0 mg
Sodium . . . . 467 mg
Carbohydrate . . . . . . 70 g
    Dietary Fiber . . . . . . 2 g
    Sugars . . . . 40 g
Protein . . . . 6 g

*I*ndex

ALPHABETICAL LIST OF RECIPES

Turkey Breakfast Sausage
  Patties, 66
Turkey Sloppy Joes, 67
Turnip Greens with Bottoms, 112

Vegetable Beef Skillet, 48

Vegetable Soup with Noodles,
  143
Vegetarian Bean Stew, 144

Willa's Lasagna, 49

SUBJECT INDEX

About the American Diabetes Association

The American Diabetes Association is the nationís leading voluntary health organization supporting diabetes research, information, and advocacy. Its mission is to prevent and cure diabetes and to improve the lives of all people affected by diabetes. The American Diabetes Association is the leading publisher of comprehensive diabetes information. Its huge library of practical and authoritative books for people with diabetes covers every aspect of self-care—cooking and nutrition, fitness, weight control, medications, complications, emotional issues, and general self-care.

To order American Diabetes Association books: Call 1-800-232-6733. Or log on to http://store.diabetes.org (Do not use www when typing in the web address.)

To join the American Diabetes Association: Call 1-800-806-7801. www.diabetes.org/membership

For more information about diabetes or ADA programs and services: Call 1-800-342-2383. E-mail: Customerservice@diabetes.org or log on to www.diabetes.org

To locate an ADA/NCQA Recognized Provider of quality diabetes care in your area: www.ncqa.org/dprp/

To find an ADA Recognized Education Program in your area: Call 1-888-232-0822. www.diabetes.org/recognition/education.asp

To join the fight to increase funding for diabetes research, end discrimination, and improve insurance coverage: Call 1-800-342-2383. www.diabetes.org/advocacy

To find out how you can get involved with the programs in your community: Call 1-800-342-2383. See below for program Web addresses.

- *American Diabetes Month:* Educational activities aimed at those diagnosed with diabetes—month of November. www.diabetes.org/ADM

- *American Diabetes Alert:* Annual public awareness campaign to find the undiagnosed—held the fourth Tuesday in March. www.diabetes.org/alert

- *The Diabetes Assistance & Resources Program (DAR):* diabetes awareness program targeted to the Latino community. www.diabetes.org/DAR

- *African American Program:* diabetes awareness program targeted to the African American community. www.diabetes.org/africanamerican

- *Awakening the Spirit: Pathways to Diabetes Prevention & Control:* diabetes awareness program targeted to the Native American community. www.diabetes.org/awakening

To find out about an important research project regarding type 2 diabetes: www.diabetes.org/ada/research.asp

To obtain information on making a planned gift or charitable bequest: Call 1-888-700-7029. www.diabetes.org/ada/plan.asp

To make a donation or memorial contribution: Call 1-800-342-2383. www.diabetes.org/ada/cont.asp